CW01103061

THE TEST CRICKETER'S ALMANAC

Jason Woolgar

Eric Dobby Publishing

© Eric Dobby Publishing 1995
© Text Jason Woolgar 1995

Published by Eric Dobby Publishing Ltd,
12 Warnford Road, Orpington, Kent BR6 6LW

All rights reserved. No part of this book may be reproduced, stored in a retrieval system now known or yet to be invented, or transmitted in any form or by any means, mechanical or electrical, photocopied or recorded without the express written permission of the publishers except by a reviewer wishing to quote brief passages in a review either written or broadcast.

A catalogue record of this book is available from the British Library.

ISBN 1-85882-043 X

Typeset in Times by Kevin O'Connor, Poole
Printed and bound in Great Britain by
BPC Hazell Books Ltd
A member of
The British Printing Company Ltd

CONTENTS

Dedication and Acknowledgements	4
Foreword by Dermot Reeve	5
Introduction	7
Test Match Records	9
Test Match Results Feb 94 - Feb 95	9
Test Match Results 1877-1995	10
Most Appearances in Test Match Cricket	11
Leading Test Match Run Scorers	12
Highest Individual Test Scores	13
Highest Test Partnerships	14
Leading Test Match Wicket Takers	16
Best Bowling in a Test Match Innings	17
Most Dismissals by a Wicket-Keeper	18
Most Test Match Catches	19
Coopers & Lybrand World Ratings	20
Test Batsmen	20
Test Bowlers	21
Player Profiles	22

This book is dedicated to

Karen Woolgar & Steve Avis

ACKNOWLEDGMENTS

I would like to thank Coopers and Lybrand for allowing me to use their ratings in this book. I am especially indebted to Gordon Vince who supplied both the ranking tables and each player's individual rating.

I am also most grateful to Patrick Eagar who supplied all the photographs for this publication.

Foreword
by Dermot Reeve

As a cricket captain I would love to have any statistical information I required totally at my disposal.

Imagine being able to have more than scoresheets or the pages of Wisden to help analyse an opponent. Being able to note, for example, that a player seems to get dismissed regularly by spin may be helpful in match tactics but scoresheets do not tell where the player may have been caught. Or for another matter, if he had struggled to score runs against his dismisser prior to the fall of his wicket.

The context of the match at the point of dismissal, condition of the wicket (eg, moisture levels), and a complete breakdown of a batsmans success against opposition bowlers would be a wonderful tool to have for pre-match meetings.

Unfortunately it will never happen. The complexity of this great game cricket would require hours of constant analysis and expensive machinery in order to prepare such details. Each match would carry dozens of pages of statistics and still not be able to tell quite the whole truth.

An area which I believe is under analysis is how quickly a batsman scores his runs when his side is attempting to win a match. It is vital to have a sound defensive technique which is imperative in trying to save Test matches but getting runs on the board and quick runs are a key to winning. It would also be useful to see a players records broken down to ascertain whether he is more successful on home soil or as a tourist.

Wickets vary so much around the world but the greats perform in any conditions. Sunil Gavasker's record in the West Indies is outstanding compared to other fine Indian batsmen. Terry Alderman's bowling in England is in total contrast to his performances in the West Indies where conditions don't suit his style as much.

Unfortunately Don Bradman only played his cricket in Australia and England! How great it would have been to see him perform on the spinning pitches of the sub-continent or lively West Indian tracks.

On a domestic level in England a batsmans home pitches may be superb for batting compared to that of another country. Surely his average will be more inflated than his less fortunate rival.

I believe averages show a general worth of a player but do not paint the full picture. One thing is for certain, statistics make fascinating reading and provoke lively debate the World over.

INTRODUCTION

During the last year Test match cricket has witnessed the departure of three of its favoured sons, with Allan Border, Kapil Dev and Graham Gooch all hanging up their spikes.

Of the three, Allan Border has enjoyed the greatest success, as his numerous Test match records testify. He has scored more runs (11174), played more matches (156), and recorded more innings of 50 or more (90) than any other Test cricketer. His 153 consecutive appearances, 156 catches and 93 matches as captain also remain Test match records. He is the only player to score 150 in each innings of a Test match (150* & 153), accomplishing this feat against Pakistan in 1979-80

Even though these records indicate a phenomenal career, a list of statistical accomplishments alone does not do justice either to Border the cricketer or to Border the man. The fact that his leadership and determined approach has turned an Australian team, in total disarray when he took the helm, into one of the very best sides in international cricket, speaks volumes for his character.

Adversity has always brought out the best in Border; his resolve and skill, and he has an abundance of both, were often all that stood between his beloved Australia and defeat. His two innings against the West Indies, at Port-of-Spain in 1983-84, best encapsulate this: he batted for a total of 634 minutes and 535 balls for 98* and 100* to avoid defeat.

His indomitable spirit and spectacular achievements should ensure that he is remembered as the greatest ever servant of Australian cricket and, in my opinion, the greatest player of all time.

The last of the mighty all-rounders, Kapil Dev, was originally compared unfavourably with the trio of Ian Botham, Richard Hadlee and Imran Khan, but he retired with a career that, statistically at least, surpassed them all. He is the only player to take 400 Test wickets and score 5000 Test runs, and his final tally of 434 wickets is a Test match record, surpassing the 431 taken by Richard Hadlee. A remarkable feat given the unhelpful Indian pitches on which he often had to bowl. He took 5 wickets in an innings on 23 occasions and his 9-83 against the West Indies in 1983-84 is the 8th best Test performance of all time.

If his bowling deteriorated slightly towards the end of his career his batting talents were still very much in evidence as recently as 1992-93, when he scored a typically dashing 129 against the South Africans. It was his 8th and final Test match century which, combined with his 27 fifties, proved what a dangerous attacking batsman he could be. When you add the 64 Test catches in his career record you suspect that the Indians will have to wait a very long time to find another cricketer with as much ability and heart as Kapil Dev.

Graham Gooch has become an unlikely hero, transforming a mediocre Test career into a glorious procession of runs and centuries. Until he was appointed England captain in 1989-90 Gooch had registered just 8 centuries in 73 Test matches, at an average of just over 36. When he retired in 1994-95 he had dramatically improved these figures, scoring a remarkable 8900 runs, the 3rd highest in Test match history, at an average of 42.58 and including 20 centuries. Although as captain he found it difficult to inspire his team-mates to his own great heights, his personal contributions with the bat were magnificent.

In 1990 he reached the pinnacle of his career, recording the 8th highest Test score of all time (333 against India at Lord's) and becoming the first player to score 1000 Test runs in an English season. His match aggregate of 456 runs in the Lord's game is the highest for a single Test, and his total of 752 runs against India is a record for a three-match series.

Of his many other outstanding innings his finest probably came in 1991 at Headingley, when his unbeaten 154 secured England's first home Test victory against the West Indies since 1969. It is this leadership from the front for which Gooch should be remembered, and although many of England's performances were poor under his captaincy they would have been much worse without his defiant and often single-handed heroics.

As in the first edition, the cricketers I have included in this book are a personal choice; my only stipulation was that they must have played in a Test match within the last 12 months. Those who have recently retired from international cricket are included if they meet this requirement. You will therefore find both Border and Gooch featured but not Javed Miandad, who has not played since the publication of the first edition.

All averages and Coopers and Lybrand ratings are correct up to and including the third Test match between Zimbabwe and Pakistan played at Harare in February 1995.

Jason Woolgar

TEST MATCH RESULTS
FEB 94 - FEB 95

Australia v South Africa Dec 93 - Feb 94
Melbourne   Match drawn
Sydney   South Africa won by 5 runs
Adelaide   Australia won by 191 runs

India v Sri Lanka Jan 94 - Feb 94
Lucknow   India won by an innings and 119 runs
Bangalore   India won by an innings and 95 runs
Ahmedabad   India won by an innings and 17 runs

New Zealand v Pakistan Feb 94
Auckland   Pakistan won by 5 wickets
Wellington   Pakistan won by an innings and 12 runs
Christchurch New Zealand won by 5 wickets

West Indies v England Feb 94 - Apr 94
Kingston   West Indies won by 8 wickets
Georgetown   West Indies won by an innings and 44 runs
Port of Spain West Indies won by 147 runs
Bridgetown   England won by 208 runs
St John's   Match drawn

South Africa v Australia Mar 94
Johannesburg South Africa won by 197 runs
Cape Town   Australia won by 9 wickets
Durban   Match drawn

New Zealand v India Mar 94
Hamilton   Match drawn

England v New Zealand June 94
Trent Bridge England won by an innings and 90 runs
Lord's   Match drawn
Old Trafford Match drawn

England v South Africa July 94 - Aug 94
Lord's   South Africa won by 356 runs
Headingley Match drawn
The Oval   England won by 8 wickets

Sri Lanka v Pakistan Aug 94
Colombo   Pakistan won by 301 runs
Kandy   Pakistan won by an innings and 52 runs

Pakistan v Australia Sept 94 - Nov 94
Karachi   Pakistan won by 1 wicket
Rawalpindi Match drawn
Lahore   Match drawn

Zimbabwe v Sri Lanka Oct 94
Harare   Match drawn

Bulawayo	Match drawn
Harare	Match drawn

India v West Indies Nov 94 - Dec 94
Bombay	India won by 96 runs
Nagpur	Match drawn
Chandigarh	West Indies won by 243 runs

South Africa v New Zealand Nov 94 - Jan 95
Johannesburg	New Zealand won by 137 runs
Durban	South Africa won by 8 wickets
Cape Town	South Africa won by 7 wickets

Australia v England Nov 94 - Feb 95
Brisbane	Australia won by 184 runs
Melbourne	Australia won by 295 runs
Sydney	Match drawn
Adelaide	England won by 106 runs
Perth	Australia won by 329 runs

South Africa v Pakistan Jan 95
Johannesburg	South Africa won by 324 runs

New Zealand v West Indies Feb 95
Christchurch	Match drawn
Wellington	West Indies won by an innings and 322 runs

Zimbabwe v Pakistan Feb 95
Harare	Zimbabwe won by an innings and 64 runs
Bulawayo	Pakistan won by 8 wickets
Harare	Pakistan won by 99 runs

TEST MATCH RESULTS
1877-1995

	Tests	Won	Drawn	Lost	Tied
Australia	547	225	166	154	2
England	712	244	266	202	0
India	292	53	141	97	1
New Zealand	234	33	105	96	0
Pakistan	221	59	113	49	0
South Africa	193	46	65	82	0
Sri Lanka	58	4	27	27	0
West Indies	310	121	115	73	1
Zimbabwe	13	1	6	6	0

MOST APPEARANCES IN TEST MATCH CRICKET

Player	Team	Tests	Aus	Eng	Ind	NZ	Pak	SA	SL	WI	Zim
A.R. Border	Aus	156	-	47	20	23	22	6	7	31	0
Kapil Dev	Ind	131	20	27	-	10	29	4	14	25	2
S.M. Gavaskar	Ind	125	20	38	-	9	24	0	7	27	0
Javed Miandad	Pak	124	25	22	28	18	-	0	12	16	3
I.V.A. Richards	WI	121	34	36	28	7	16	0	0	-	0
G.A. Gooch	Eng	118	42	-	19	15	10	3	3	26	0
D.I. Gower	Eng	117	42	-	24	13	17	0	2	19	0
D.B. Vengsarkar	Ind	116	24	26	-	11	22	0	8	25	0
D.L. Haynes	WI	116	33	36	19	10	16	1	1	-	0
M.C. Cowdrey	Eng	114	43	-	8	18	10	14	0	21	0
C.H. Lloyd	WI	110	29	34	28	8	11	0	0	-	0
G. Boycott	Eng	108	38	-	13	15	6	7	0	29	0
C.G. Greenidge	WI	108	29	32	23	10	14	0	0	-	0
I.T. Botham	Eng	102	36	-	14	15	14	0	3	20	0

LEADING TEST MATCH RUN SCORERS

Player	Team	Mat	Inns	NO	Runs	HS	Avg	100	50
A.R. Border	Aus	156	265	44	11174	205	50.56	27	63
S.M. Gavaskar	Ind	125	214	16	10122	236*	51.12	34	45
G.A. Gooch	Eng	118	215	6	8900	333	42.58	20	46
Javed Miandad	Pak	124	189	21	8832	280*	52.57	23	43
I.V.A. Richards	WI	121	182	12	8540	291	50.23	24	45
D.I. Gower	Eng	117	204	18	8231	215	44.25	18	39
G. Boycott	Eng	108	193	23	8114	246*	47.72	22	42
G.S. Sobers	WI	93	160	21	8032	365*	57.78	26	30
M.C. Cowdrey	Eng	114	188	15	7624	182	44.06	22	38
C.G. Greenidge	WI	108	185	16	7558	226	44.72	19	34
C.H. Lloyd	WI	110	175	14	7515	242*	46.67	19	39
D.L. Haynes	WI	116	202	25	7487	184	42.29	18	39
W.R. Hammond	Eng	85	140	16	7249	336*	58.45	22	24
G.S. Chappell	Aus	87	151	19	7110	247*	53.86	24	31
D.G. Bradman	Aus	52	80	10	6996	334	99.94	29	13
L. Hutton	Eng	79	138	15	6971	364	56.67	19	33
D.C. Boon	Aus	97	175	20	6959	200	44.89	20	30
D.B. Vengsarkar	Ind	116	185	22	6868	166	42.13	17	35
K.F. Barrington	Eng	82	131	15	6806	256	58.67	20	35
R.B. Kanhai	WI	79	137	6	6227	256	47.53	15	28
R.N. Harvey	Aus	79	137	10	6149	205	48.41	21	24
G.R. Viswanath	Ind	91	155	10	6080	222	41.93	14	35

The Test Cricketer's Almanac

HIGHEST INDIVIDUAL TEST SCORES

375	B.C. Lara	WI v Eng	St John's	1993-94
365*	G.S. Sobers	WI v Pak	Kingston	1957-58
364	L. Hutton	Eng v Aus	The Oval	1938
337	Hanif Mohammad	Pak v WI	Bridgetown	1957-58
336*	W.R. Hammond	Eng v NZ	Auckland	1932-33
334	D.G. Bradman	Aus v Eng	Headingley	1930
333	G.A. Gooch	Eng v Ind	Lord's	1990
325	A. Sandham	Eng v WI	Kingston	1929-30
311	R.B. Simpson	Aus v Eng	Old Trafford	1964
310*	J.H. Edrich	Eng v NZ	Headingley	1965
307	R.M. Cowper	Aus v Eng	Melbourne	1965-66
304	D.G. Bradman	Aus v Eng	Headingley	1934
302	L.G. Rowe	WI v Eng	Bridgetown	1973-74
299*	D.G. Bradman	Aus v SA	Adelaide	1931-32
299	M.D. Crowe	NZ v SL	Wellington	1990-91
291	I.V.A. Richards	WI v Eng	The Oval	1976
287	R.E. Foster	Eng v Aus	Sydney	1903-04
285*	P.B.H. May	Eng v WI	Edgbaston	1957
280*	Javed Miandad	Pak v Ind	Hyderabad	1982-83
278	D.C.S. Compton	Eng v Pak	Trent Bridge	1954
277	B.C. Lara	WI v Aus	Sydney	1992-93
274	R.G. Pollock	SA v Aus	Durban	1969-70
274	Zaheer Abbas	Pak v Eng	Edgbaston	1971
271	Javed Miandad	Pak v NZ	Auckland	1988-89
270*	G.A. Headley	WI v Eng	Kingston	1934-35
270	D.G. Bradman	Aus v Eng	Melbourne	1936-37
268	G.N. Yallop	Aus v Pak	Melbourne	1983-84
267	P.A. De Silva	SL v NZ	Wellington	1990-91
266	W.H. Ponsford	Aus v Eng	The Oval	1934
266	D.L. Houghton	Zim v SL	Bulawayo	1993-94
262*	D.L. Amiss	Eng v WI	Kingston	1973-74
261	F.M.M. Worrell	WI v Eng	Trent Bridge	1950
260	C.C. Hunte	WI v Pak	Kingston	1957-58
260	Javed Miandad	Pak v Eng	The Oval	1987
259	G.M. Turner	NZ v WI	Georgetown	1971-72
258	T.W. Graveney	Eng v WI	Trent Bridge	1957
258	S.M. Nurse	WI v NZ	Christchurch	1968-69
256	R.B. Kanhai	WI v Ind	Calcutta	1958-59
256	K.F. Barrington	Eng v Aus	Old Trafford	1964
255*	D.J. McGlew	SA v NZ	Wellington	1952-53
254	D.G. Bradman	Aus v Eng	Lord's	1930
251	W.R. Hammond	Eng v Aus	Sydney	1928-29
250	K.D. Walters	Aus v NZ	Christchurch	1976-77
250	S.F.A.F. Bacchus	WI v Ind	Kanpur	1978-79

13

HIGHEST TEST PARTNERSHIPS FOR EACH WICKET

Wkt	Runs	Teams	Venue	Year	Batsmen
1st	413	Ind v NZ	Madras	1955-56	M.H. Mankad/ Pankaj Roy
2nd	451	Aus v Eng	The Oval	1934	W.H. Ponsford/ D.G. Bradman
3rd	467	NZ v SL	Wellington	1990-91	A.H. Jones/ M.D. Crowe
4th	411	Eng v WI	Birmingham	1957	P.B.H. May/ M.C. Cowdrey
5th	405	Aus v Eng	Sydney	1946-47	S.G. Barnes/ D.G. Bradman
6th	346	Aus v Eng	Melbourne	1936-37	J.H.W. Fingleton/ D.G. Bradman
7th	347	WI v Aus	Bridgetown	1954-55	D. St E. Atkinson/ C.C. Depeiza
8th	246	Eng v NZ	Lord's	1931	L.E.G. Ames/ G.O.B. Allen
9th	190	Pak v Eng	The Oval	1967	Asif Iqbal/ Intikhab Alam
10th	151	NZ v Pak	Auckland	1972-73	B.F Hastings/ R.O. Collinge

TOTAL HIGHEST TEST PARTNERSHIPS

Runs	Wkt	Teams	Venue	Year	Batsmen
467	3rd	NZ v SL	Wellington	1990-91	A.H. Jones/ M.D. Crowe
451	2nd	Aus v Eng	The Oval	1934	W.H. Ponsford/ D.G. Bradman
451	3rd	Pak v Ind	Hyderabad	1982-83	Mudassar Nazar/ Javed Miandad
446	2nd	WI v Pak	Kingston	1957-58	C.C. Hunte/ G.S. Sobers
413	1st	Ind v NZ	Madras	1955-56	M.H. Mankad/ Pankaj Roy
411	4th	Eng v WI	Edgbaston	1957	P.B.H. May/ M.C. Cowdrey
405	5th	Aus v Eng	Sydney	1946-47	S.G. Barnes/ D.G. Bradman
399	4th	WI v Eng	Bridgetown	1959-60	G.S. Sobers/ F.M.M. Worrell
397	3rd	Pak v SL	Faisalabad	1985-86	Qasim Omar/ Javed Miandad
388	4th	Aus v Eng	Headingley	1934	W.H. Ponsford/ D.G. Bradman
387	1st	NZ v WI	Georgetown	1971-72	G.M. Turner/ T.W. Jarvis
382	2nd	Eng v Aus	The Oval	1938	L. Hutton/ M. Leyland

382	1st	Aus v WI	Bridgetown	1964-65	W.M. Lawry/ R.B. Simpson
370	3rd	Eng v SA	Lord's	1947	W.J. Edrich/ D.C.S. Compton
369	2nd	Eng v NZ	Headingley	1965	J.H. Edrich/ K.F. Barrington
359	1st	Eng v SA	Johannesburg	1948-49	L. Hutton/ C. Washbrook
351	2nd	Eng v Aus	The Oval	1985	G.A. Gooch/ D.I. Gower
350	4th	Pak v NZ	Dunedin	1972-73	Mushtaq Mohammad/ Asif Iqbal
347	7th	WI v Aus	Bridgetown	1954-55	D. St E. Atkinson/ C.C. Depeiza
346	6th	Aus v Eng	Melbourne	1936-37	J.H.W. Fingleton/ D.G. Bradman
344*	2nd	Ind v WI	Calcutta	1978-79	S.M. Gavaskar/ D.B. Vengsarkar
341	3rd	SA v Aus	Adelaide	1963-64	E.J. Barlow/ R.G. Pollock
338	3rd	WI v Eng	Port of Spain	1953-54	E.D. Weekes/ F.M.M. Worrell
336	4th	Aus v WI	Sydney	1968-69	W.M. Lawry/ K.D. Walters
332*	5th	Aus v Eng	Headingley	1993	A.R. Border/ S.R. Waugh
331	2nd	Eng v Aus	Edgbaston	1985	R.T. Robinson/ D.I. Gower
329	1st	Aus v Eng	Trent Bridge	1989	G.R. Marsh/ M.A. Taylor
323	1st	Eng v Aus	Melbourne	1911-12	J.B. Hobbs/ W. Rhodes
322	4th	Pak v Eng	Edgbaston	1992	Javed Miandad/ Salim Malik
319	3rd	SA v Eng	Trent Bridge	1947	A. Melville/ A.D. Nourse
316[1]	3rd	Ind v Eng	Madras	1981-82	G.R. Viswanath/ Yashpal Sharma
308	7th	Pak v NZ	Lahore	1955-56	Waqar Hassan/ Imtiaz Ahmed
308	3rd	WI v Aus	St John's	1983-84	R.B. Richardson/ I.V.A. Richards
308	3rd	Eng v Ind	Lord's	1990	G.A. Gooch/ A.J. Lamb
303	3rd	WI v Eng	Trent Bridge	1976	I.V.A. Richards/ A.I. Kallicharran
303	3rd	Eng v WI	St John's	1993-94	M.A. Atherton/ R.A. Smith
301	2nd	Aus v Eng	Headingley	1948	A.R. Morris/ D.G. Bradman

[1] D.B. Vengsarkar retired hurt and was succeeded by Yashpal Sharma when the score was 99. In all 415 runs were scored for the 3rd wicket.

LEADING TEST MATCH WICKET TAKERS

Player	Team Balls	Runs	Wkts	Avg	B/B	5WI	10WM	S/R
Kapil Dev	Ind 27740	12867	434	29.64	9-83	23	2	63.91
R.J. Hadlee	NZ 21918	9611	431	22.29	9-52	36	9	50.85
I.T. Botham	Eng 21815	10878	383	28.40	8-34	27	4	56.95
M.D. Marshall	WI 17584	7876	376	20.94	7-22	22	4	46.76
Imran Khan	Pak 19458	8258	362	22.81	8-58	23	6	53.75
D.K. Lillee	Aus 18467	8493	355	23.92	7-83	23	7	52.01
R.G.D. Willis	Eng 17357	8190	325	25.20	8-43	16	0	53.40
L.R. Gibbs	WI 27115	8989	309	29.09	8-38	18	2	87.75
F.S. Trueman	Eng 15178	6625	307	21.57	8-31	17	3	49.43
D.L. Underwood	Eng 21862	7674	297	25.83	8-51	17	6	73.60
C. McDermott	Aus 15385	7697	270	28.50	8-97	13	2	56.98
B.S. Bedi	Ind 21364	7637	266	28.71	7-98	14	1	80.31
Wasim Akram	Pak 14039	6057	261	23.20	7-119	18	3	53.78
J. Garner	WI 13169	5433	259	20.97	6-56	7	0	50.84
C.A. Walsh	WI 14455	6317	255	24.77	7-37	9	2	56.68
J.B. Statham	Eng 16056	6261	252	24.84	7-39	9	1	63.71
M.A. Holding	WI 12680	5898	249	23.68	8-92	13	2	50.92
R. Benaud	Aus 19108	6704	248	27.03	7-72	16	1	77.04
G.D. McKenzie	Aus 17681	7328	246	29.78	8-71	16	3	71.87
B.S. Chandrasekhar	Ind 15963	7199	242	29.74	8-79	16	2	65.96
A.V. Bedser	Eng 15918	5876	236	24.89	7-44	15	5	67.44
Abdul Qadir	Pak 17126	7742	236	32.80	9-56	15	5	72.56
G.S. Sobers	WI 21599	7999	235	34.03	6-73	6	0	91.91
R.R. Lindwall	Aus 13650	5251	228	23.03	7-38	12	0	59.86
C.E.L. Ambrose	WI 12157	4729	224	21.11	8-45	11	3	54.27
C.V. Grimmett	Aus 14513	5231	216	24.21	7-40	21	7	67.18
M. Hughes	Aus 12285	6017	212	28.38	8-87	7	1	57.94
J.A. Snow	Eng 12021	5387	202	26.66	7-40	8	1	59.50
A.M.E. Roberts	WI 11135	5174	202	25.61	7-54	11	2	55.12
J.R. Thomson	Aus 10535	5601	200	28.00	6-46	8	0	52.67
J.C. Laker	Eng 12207	4101	193	21.24	10-53	9	3	62.31
W.W. Hall	WI 10421	5066	192	26.38	7-69	9	1	54.27
Waqar Younis	Pak 6858	3641	190	19.16	7-76	19	4	36.09
S.F. Barnes	Eng 7873	3106	189	16.43	9-103	24	7	41.65
E.A.S. Prasanna	Ind 14353	5742	189	30.38	8-76	10	2	75.94
A.K. Davidson	Aus 11587	3819	186	20.53	7-93	14	2	62.29
G.F. Lawson	Aus 11118	5501	180	30.56	8-112	11	2	61.76
Sarfraz Nawaz	Pak 13927	5798	177	32.75	9-86	4	1	78.68
G.A.R. Lock	Aus 13147	4451	174	25.58	7-35	9	3	75.55
Iqbal Qasim	Pak 13019	4807	171	28.11	7-49	8	2	76.13
K.R. Miller	Aus 10461	3906	170	22.97	7-60	7	1	61.53
H.J. Tayfield	SA 13568	4405	170	25.91	9-113	14	2	79.81
T.M. Alderman	Aus 10181	4616	170	27.15	6-47	14	1	59.88
M.H. Mankad	Ind 14686	5236	162	32.32	8-52	8	2	90.65
S.K. Warne	Aus 10612	3833	161	23.80	8-71	9	2	65.91
W.A. Johnston	Aus 11048	3826	160	23.91	6-44	7	0	69.05

BEST BOWLING IN A TEST MATCH INNINGS

10-53	J.C. Laker	Eng v Aus	Old Trafford	1956
9-28	G.A. Lohmann	Eng v SA	Johannesburg	1895-96
9-37	J.C. Laker	Eng v Aus	Old Trafford	1956
9-52	R.J. Hadlee	NZ v Aus	Brisbane	1985-86
9-56	Abdul Qadir	Pak v Eng	Lahore	1987-88
9-57	D.E. Malcolm	Eng v SA	The Oval	1994
9-69	J.M. Patel	Ind v Aus	Kanpur	1959-60
9-83	Kapil Dev	Ind v WI	Ahmedabad	1983-84
9-86	Sarfraz Nawaz	Pak v Aus	Melbourne	1978-79
9-95	J.M. Noreiga	WI v Ind	Port of Spain	1970-71
9-102	S.P. Gupte	Ind v WI	Kanpur	1958-59
9-103	S.F. Barnes	Eng v SA	Johannesburg	1913-14
9-113	H.J. Tayfield	SA v Eng	Johannesburg	1956-57
9-121	A.A. Mailey	Aus v Eng	Melbourne	1920-21
8-7	G.A. Lohmann	Eng v SA	Port Elizabeth	1895-96
8-11	J. Briggs	Eng v SA	Cape Town	1888-89
8-29	S.F. Barnes	Eng v SA	The Oval	1912
8-29	C.E.H. Croft	WI v Pak	Port of Spain	1976-77
8-31	F. Laver	Aus v Eng	Old Trafford	1909
8-31	F.S. Trueman	Eng v Ind	Old Trafford	1952
8-34	I.T. Botham	Eng v Pak	Lord's	1978
8-35	G.A. Lohmann	Eng v Aus	Sydney	1886-87
8-38	L.R. Gibbs	WI v Ind	Bridgetown	1961-62
8-43	A.E. Trott	Aus v Eng	Adelaide	1894-95
8-43	H. Verity	Eng v Aus	Lord's	1934
8-43	R.G.D. Willis	Eng v Aus	Headingley	1981
8-45	C.E.L. Ambrose	WI v Eng	Bridgetown	1989-90
8-51	D.L. Underwood	Eng v Pak	Lord's	1974
8-52	M.H. Mankad	Ind v Pak	Delhi	1952-53
8-53	G.B. Lawrence	SA v NZ	Johannesburg	1961-62
8-53	R.A.L. Massie	Aus v Eng	Lord's	1972
8-55	M.H. Mankad	Ind v Eng	Madras	1951-52
8-56	S.F. Barnes	Eng v SA	Johannesburg	1913-14
8-58	G.A. Lohmann	Eng v Aus	Sydney	1891-92
8-58	Imran Khan	Pak v SL	Lahore	1981-82
8-59	C. Blythe	Eng v SA	Headingley	1907
8-59	A.A. Mallett	Aus v Pak	Adelaide	1972-73
8-60	Imran Khan	Pak v Ind	Karachi	1982-83
8-61	N.D. Hirwani	Ind v WI	Madras	1987-88
8-65	H. Trumble	Aus v Eng	The Oval	1902
8-68	W. Rhodes	Eng v Aus	Melbourne	1903-04
8-69	H.J. Tayfield	SA v Eng	Durban	1956-57
8-69	Sikander Bakht	Pak v Ind	Delhi	1979-80
8-70	S.J. Snooke	SA v Eng	Johannesburg	1905-06
8-71	G.D. McKenzie	Aus v WI	Melbourne	1968-69
8-71	S.K. Warne	Aus v Eng	Brisbane	1994-95
8-72	S. Venkataraghavan	Ind v NZ	Delhi	1964-65
8-75	N.D. Hirwani	Ind v WI	Madras	1987-88
8-75	A.R.C. Fraser	Eng v WI	Bridgetown	1993-94

MOST DISMISSALS BY A WICKET-KEEPER IN TEST MATCHES

Player	Team	Tests	Cat	St	Total	DPM
R.W. Marsh	Aus	96	343	12	355	3.69
P.J.L. Dujon	WI	81	267	5	272*	3.35
A.P.E. Knott	Eng	95	250	19	269	2.83
I.A. Healy	Aus	69	222	16	238	3.44
Wasim Bari	Pak	81	201	27	228	2.81
T.G. Evans	Eng	91	173	46	219	2.40
S.M.H. Kirmani	Ind	88	160	38	198	2.25
D.L. Murray	WI	62	181	8	189	3.04
A.T.W. Grout	Aus	51	163	24	187	3.66
I.D.S. Smith	NZ	63	168	8	176	2.79
R.W. Taylor	Eng	57	167	7	174	3.05
J.H.B. Waite	SA	50	124	17	141	2.82
W.A.S. Oldfield	Aus	54	78	52	130	2.40
K.S. More	Ind	49	110	20	130	2.65
J.M. Parks	Eng	46	103	11	114#	2.47
Salim Yousuf	Pak	32	91	13	104	3.25

* Includes 2 catches in 2 Tests when not keeping wicket # Includes 2 catches in 3 Tests when not keeping wicket

MOST TEST MATCH CATCHES

Player	Team	Cat	Aus	Eng	Ind	NZ	Pak	SA	SL	WI	Zim
A.R. Border	Aus	156	-	57	14	31	22	5	8	19	0
G.S. Chappell	Aus	122	-	61	5	18	22	0	0	16	0
I.V.A. Richards	WI	122	24	29	39	7	23	0	0	-	0
M.C. Cowdrey	Eng	120	40	-	11	15	11	22	0	21	0
I.T. Botham	Eng	120	57	-	14	14	14	0	2	19	0
W.R. Hammond	Eng	110	43	-	6	9	0	30	0	22	0
R.B. Simpson	Aus	110	-	30	21	0	3	27	0	29	0
G.S. Sobers	WI	109	27	40	27	11	4	0	0	-	0
S.M. Gavaskar	Ind	108	19	35	-	11	19	0	7	17	0
I.M. Chappell	Aus	105	-	31	17	16	6	11	0	24	0
G.A. Gooch	Eng	103	29	-	21	13	7	1	4	28	0

The Test Cricketer's Almanac

COOPERS & LYBRAND WORLD RATINGS - TEST BATSMEN

Rank	Player	Team	Rating
1	J.C. Adams	West Indies	923
2	Inzamam-ul-Haq	Pakistan	868
3	B.C. Lara	West Indies	794
4	S.R. Tendulkar	India	774
5=	S.R. Waugh	Australia	758
	G.P. Thorpe	England	758
7	M.J. Slater	Australia	755
8	Salim Malik	Pakistan	708
9	D.L. Haynes	West Indies	698
10	M.A. Atherton	England	693
11	G. Kirsten	South Africa	670
12	R.B. Richardson	West Indies	664
13	A.J. Stewart	England	659
14	D.C. Boon	Australia	658
15	M.E. Waugh	Australia	652
16	G.A. Hick	England	649
17	A. Flower	Zimbabwe	636
18	W.J. Cronje	South Africa	625
19	M. Azharuddin	India	618
20	H.P. Tillekeratne	Sri Lanka	616
21	M.A. Taylor	Australia	613
22	G.A. Gooch	England	606
23=	M.D. Crowe	New Zealand	603
	N.S. Sidhu	India	603
25	D.L. Houghton	Zimbabwe	598
26	V.G. Kambli	India	590 *
27	Aamir Sohail	Pakistan	583
28	Saeed Anwar	Pakistan	582
29	B.M. McMillan	South Africa	574
30	Shoaib Mohammad	Pakistan	567
31=	A.H. Jones	New Zealand	563
	A.D.R. Campbell	Zimbabwe	563
33	C.L. Hooper	West Indies	559
34	K.C. Wessels	Australia/ South Africa	554
35	S.P. Fleming	New Zealand	546 *
36	P.A. de Silva	Sri Lanka	544
37	J.N. Rhodes	South Africa	536
38	Javed Miandad	Pakistan	531
39	K.L.T. Arthurton	West Indies	528
40	A. Ranatunga	Sri Lanka	517
41	Ijaz Ahmed	Pakistan	514
42	B.A. Young	New Zealand	513
43	R.A. Smith	England	508
44	P.N. Kirsten	South Africa	507
45	J.R. Murray	West Indies	505
46=	I.A. Healy	Australia	504
	D.J. Cullinan	South Africa	504
48	S.A. Thomson	New Zealand	495
49=	S.V. Manjrekar	India	487
	A.C. Hudson	South Africa	487

The Test Cricketer's Almanac

COOPERS & LYBRAND WORLD RATINGS - TEST BOWLERS

Rank	Player	Team	Rating
1	C.E.L. Ambrose	West Indies	870
2	S.K. Warne	Australia	860
3	Waqar Younis	Pakistan	859
4	H.H. Streak	Zimbabwe	819 *
5	P.S. de Villiers	South Africa	803
6	A.R. Kumble	India	797
7	C.A. Walsh	West Indies	767
8	Wasim Akram	Pakistan	757
9	C.J. McDermott	Australia	719
10	Venkatapathy Raju	India	705
11	K.C.G. Benjamin	West Indies	688 *
12	A.A. Donald	South Africa	686
13	B.M. McMillan	South Africa	669
14	A.R.C. Fraser	England	639
15	D. Gough	England	588 *
16	M.G. Hughes	Australia	582
17	P.A.J. DeFreitas	England	553
18	D.K. Morrison	New Zealand	532
19	C.R. Matthews	South Africa	525 *
20	M. Prabhakar	India	523
21	W.K.M. Benjamin	West Indies	517
22	M. Muralitharan	Sri Lanka	509
23	D.E. Malcolm	England	491
24	K.P.J. Warnaweera	Sri Lanka	454 *
25	S.B. Doull	New Zealand	453 *
26	P.R. Reiffel	Australia	446 *
27	C.C. Lewis	England	445
28	Mushtaq Ahmed	Pakistan	413 *
29	J. Srinath	India	406 *
30	T.B.A. May	Australia	405
31	D.W. Fleming	Australia	398 *
32	P.C.R. Tufnell	England	393
33	D.H. Brain	Zimbabwe	367 *
34	C.P.H. Ramanayake	Sri Lanka	363 *
35	D.J. Nash	New Zealand	359 *
36	R.K. Chauhan	India	357 *
37	Aamir Nazir	Pakistan	356 *
38	Aqib Javed	Pakistan	345 *
39	M.E. Waugh	Australia	335 *
40	G.D. McGrath	Australia	324 *
41	S.D. Anurasiri	Sri Lanka	320 *
42	Tausif Ahmed	Pakistan	314
43	W. Watson	New Zealand	307 *
44	D.N. Patel	New Zealand	298 *
45	S.R. Waugh	Australia	295
46	G.J. Whittall	Zimbabwe	294 *
47	C.L. Hooper	West Indies	293 *
48	R.A. Harper	West Indies	287 *
49	B. Strang	Zimbabwe	286 *
50	A.R. Caddick	England	264 *

AAMIR SOHAIL

Full name: Aamir Sohail
Born: 14/09/66 Lahore, Pakistan
Country: Pakistan
Left-hand opening batsman - Left-arm slow bowler
Test debut: 04/06/92 v England Edgbaston, Birmingham

Test Career Record: *Batting & Fielding*								
Mat	Inns	N/O	Runs	H/S	Avg	100s	50s	Cat
23	43	1	1508	205	35.90	2	10	26
Test Career Record: *Bowling*								
Balls	Runs	Wkts	Avg	Best	5WI	10WM		BPW
525	295	8	36.87	2-5	0	0		65.62

Overseas tours: Aus 91/92, 92/93, Eng 92, NZ 92/93, 93/94, WI 92/93, SA 92/93, 94/95, Zim 92/93, 94/95, SL 94/95, Sharjah 90/91, 91/92, 93/94, WC: Aus & NZ 91/92, Pak B: Zim 86/87, Pak A: SL 90/91

Test matches: Eng 92 (5), NZ 92/93 (1), WI 92/93 (2), Zim 93/94 (3), NZ 93/94 (3), SL 94/95 (2), Aus 94/95 (3), SA 94/95 (1), Zim 94/95 (3)

Highest score against each country:			100s	50s
Australia	105	Lahore 94/95	1	2
England	205	Old Trafford 92	1	1
New Zealand	78	Auckland 93/94	0	2
South Africa	23	Johannesburg 94/95	0	0
Sri Lanka	74	Kandy 94/95	0	2
West Indies	55	Port of Spain 92/93	0	1
Zimbabwe	63	Karachi 93/94	0	2

Coopers & Lybrand world rating (batting): 27 (583)

Player Profiles

JIMMY ADAMS

Full name: James Clive Adams
Born: 09/01/68 Port Maria, Jamaica
Country: West Indies
Left-hand middle order batsman - Left-arm slow bowler - Wicket-Keeper
Test debut: 18/04/92 v South Africa - Kensington Oval, Bridgetown

Test Career Record: *Batting & Fielding*								
Mat	Inns	N/O	Runs	H/S	Avg	100s	50s	Cat
14	21	6	1296	174*	86.40	4	6	17

Test Career Record: *Bowling*							
Balls	Runs	Wkts	Avg	Best	5WI	10WM	BPW
741	395	9	43.88	4-43	0	0	82.33

Overseas tours: Aus 92/93, SA 92/93, Ind 93/94, 94/95, SL 93/94, NZ 94/95, Sharjah 93/94, Young WI: Aus 88, Zim 86/87, 89/90, RW: Eng 93

Test matches: SA 91/92 (1), Aus 92/93 (3), Eng 93/94 (5), Ind 94/95 (3), NZ 94/95 (2)

Highest score against each country:			100s	50s
Australia	77*	Sydney 92/93	0	1
England	137	Georgetown 93/94	1	2
India	174*	Chandigarh 94/95	2	2
New Zealand	151	Wellington 94/95	1	0
South Africa	79*	Bridgetown 91/92	0	1

Coopers & Lybrand world rating (batting): 1 (923)

CURTLY AMBROSE

Full name: Curtly Elconn Lynwall Ambrose
Born: 21/09/63   Swetes Village, Antigua
Country: West Indies
Right-arm fast bowler - Left-hand lower order batsman
Test debut: 02/04/88 v Pakistan - Bourda, Georgetown

Test Career Record: *Batting & Fielding*								
Mat	Inns	N/O	Runs	H/S	Avg	100s	50s	Cat
50	71	13	713	53	12.29	0	1	11
Test Career Record: *Bowling*								
Balls	Runs	Wkts	Avg	Best	5WI	10WM		BPW
12157	4729	224	21.11	8-45	11	3		54.27

Overseas tours: Eng 88, 91, Aus 88/89, 91/92, 92/93, Ind 89/90, 93/94, Pak 90/91, 91/92, SA 92/93, SL 93/94, NZ 94/95, Sharjah 88/89, 89/90, 91/92, 93/94, WC: Aus & NZ 91/92

Test matches: Pak 87/88 (3), Eng 88 (5), Aus 88/89 (5), Ind 88/89 (4), Eng 89/90 (3), Pak 90/91 (3), Aus 90/91 (5), Eng 91 (5), SA 91/92 (1), Aus 92/93 (5), Pak 92/93 (3), SL 93/94 (1), Eng 93/94 (5), NZ 94/95 (2)

Best bowling against each country:			5WI	10WM
Australia	7-25	Perth 92/93	4	1
England	8-45	Bridgetown 89/90	5	2
India	3-66	Bridgetown 88/89	0	0
New Zealand	3-57	Christchurch 94/95	0	0
Pakistan	5-35	Lahore 90/91	1	0
South Africa	6-34	Bridgetown 91/92	1	0
Sri Lanka	3-14	Moratuwa 93/94	0	0

Coopers & Lybrand world rating (bowling): 1 (870)

Player Profiles

KEITH ARTHURTON

Full name: Keith Lloyd Thomas Arthurton
Born: 21/02/65   Charlestown, Nevis
Country: West Indies
Left-hand middle order batsman - Left-arm slow bowler
Test debut: 21/07/88 v England - Headingley, Leeds

Test Career Record: *Batting & Fielding*								
Mat	*Inns*	*N/O*	*Runs*	*H/S*	*Avg*	*100s*	*50s*	*Cat*
25	39	5	1149	157*	33.79	2	7	14

Test Career Record: *Bowling*							
Balls	*Runs*	*Wkts*	*Avg*	*Best*	*5WI*	*10WM*	*BPW*
234	89	0	-	-	-	-	-

Overseas tours: Eng 88, Aus 88/89, 91/92, 92/93, Ind 89/90, 93/94, 94/95, Pak 91/92, SL 93/94, NZ 94/95, Sharjah 88/89, 89/90, 91/92, 93/94, WC: Aus & NZ 91/92, RW: Eng 93

Test matches: Eng 88 (1), Ind 88/89 (4), SA 91/92 (1), Aus 92/93 (5), Pak 92/93 (3), SL 93/94 (1), Eng 93/94 (5), Ind 94/95 (3), NZ 94/95 (2)

Highest score against each country:			100s	50s
Australia	157*	Brisbane 92/93	1	2
England	126	Kingston 93/94	1	1
India	70*	Chandigarh 94/95	0	1
New Zealand	70	Wellington 94/95	0	1
Pakistan	56	Bridgetown 92/93	0	1
South Africa	59	Bridgetown 91/92	0	1
Sri Lanka	0	Moratuwa 93/94	0	0

Coopers & Lybrand world rating (batting): 39 (528)

ASIF MUJTABA

Full name: Asif Mujtaba
Born: 04/11/67   Karachi, Pakistan
Country: Pakistan
Left-hand middle order batsman - Left-arm slow bowler
Test debut: 07/11/86 v West Indies - Gaddafi Stadium, Lahore

Test Career Record: Batting & Fielding								
Mat	Inns	N/O	Runs	H/S	Avg	100s	50s	Cat
21	35	3	762	65*	23.81	0	7	17
Test Career Record: Bowling								
Balls	Runs	Wkts	Avg	Best	5WI	10WM		BPW
264	152	2	76.00	1-0	0	0		132.00

Overseas tours: Ind 86/87, Aus 86/87, 92/93, Eng 87, 92, WI 92/93, NZ 92/93, 93/94, SA 92/93, 94/95, Zim 92/93, 94/95, SL 94/95, Sharjah 86/87, 92/93, 93/94, Pak B: Zim 86/87, 90/91

Test matches: WI 86/87 (2), Eng 87/88 (1), Eng 92 (5), NZ 92/93 (1), WI 92/93 (3), Zim 93/94 (3), NZ 93/94 (2), SL 94/95 (2), SA 94/95 (1), Zim 94/95 (1)

Highest score against each country:			100s	50s
England	59	Lord's 92	0	3
New Zealand	11	Hamilton 92/93	0	0
South Africa	26	Johannesburg 94/95	0	0
Sri Lanka	44	Colombo 94/95	0	0
West Indies	59	St John's 92/93	0	1
Zimbabwe	65*	Lahore 93/94	0	3

Coopers & Lybrand world rating (batting): 68 (357)

Player Profiles

MICHAEL ATHERTON

Full name: Michael Andrew Atherton
Born: 23/03/68   Manchester, Lancashire, England
Country: England
Right-hand opening batsman - Leg break bowler
Test debut: 10/08/89 v Australia - Trent Bridge, Nottingham

Test Career Record: *Batting & Fielding*								
Mat	Inns	N/O	Runs	H/S	Avg	100s	50s	Cat
45	84	1	3324	151	40.04	7	23	34
Test Career Record: *Bowling*								
Balls	Runs	Wkts	Avg	Best	5WI	10WM		BPW
366	282	1	282.00	1-60	0	0		366.00

Overseas tours: Aus 90/91, 94/95, NZ 90/91, Ind 92/93, SL 92/93, WI 93/94, Eng A: Zim & Ken 89/90

Test matches: Aus 89 (2), NZ 90 (3), Ind 90 (3), Aus 90/91 (5), WI 91 (5), Pak 92 (3), Ind 92/93 (1), SL 92/93 (1), Aus 93 (6), WI 93/94 (5), NZ 94 (3), SA 94 (3), Aus 94/95 (5)

Highest score against each country:			100s	50s
Australia	105	Sydney 90/91	1	11
India	131	Old Trafford 90	1	3
New Zealand	151	Trent Bridge 90	3	3
Pakistan	76	Headingley 92	0	2
South Africa	99	Headingley 94	0	2
Sri Lanka	13	Colombo 92/93	0	0
West Indies	144	Georgetown 93/94	2	2

Coopers & Lybrand world rating (batting): 10 (693)

MOHAMMAD AZHARUDDIN

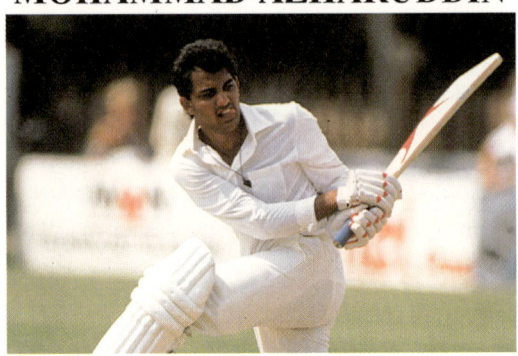

Full name: Mohammad Azharuddin
Born: 08/02/63   Hyderabad, India
Country: India
Right-hand middle order batsman - Right-arm medium bowler
Test debut: 31/12/84 v England - Eden Gardens, Calcutta

Test Career Record: *Batting & Fielding*								
Mat	*Inns*	*N/O*	*Runs*	*H/S*	*Avg*	*100s*	*50s*	*Cat*
65	94	4	4198	199	46.64	14	14	68

Test Career Record: *Bowling*							
Balls	*Runs*	*Wkts*	*Avg*	*Best*	*5WI*	*10WM*	*BPW*
7	12	0	-	-	-	-	-

Overseas tours: Aus 84/85, 85/86, 91/92, SL 85/86, 93/94, 94/95, Eng 86, 90, WI 89/90, NZ 89/90, 93/94, 94/95, Pak 89/90, Zim 92/93, SA 92/93, Ban 88/89, Sharjah 84/85, 85/86, 86/87, 87/88, 88/89, 89/90, 91/92, 93/94, WC: Aus & NZ 91/92, Young Ind: Zim 83/84

Test matches: Eng 84/85 (3), SL 85/86 (3), Aus 85/86 (3), Eng 86 (3), Aus 86/87 (3), SL 86/87 (1), Pak 86/87 (5), WI 87/88 (3), NZ 88/89 (3), WI 88/89 (3), Pak 89/90 (4), NZ 89/90 (3), Eng 90 (3), SL 90/91 (1), Aus 91/92 (5), Zim 92/93 (1), SA 92/93 (4), Eng 92/93 (3), Zim 92/93 (1), SL 93/94 (3), SL 93/94 (3), NZ 93/94 (1), WI 94/95 (3)

Highest score against each country:			100s	50s
Australia	106	Adelaide 91/92	1	2
England	182	Calcutta 92/93	6	3
New Zealand	192	Auckland 89/90	1	2
Pakistan	141	Calcutta 86/87	3	2
South Africa	60	Port Elizabeth 92/93	0	1
Sri Lanka	199	Kanpur 86/87	3	1
West Indies	97	Nagpur 94/95	0	3
Zimbabwe	42	Delhi 92/93	0	0

Coopers & Lybrand world rating (batting): 19 (618)

BASIT ALI

Full name: Basit Ali
Born: 13/12/70   Karachi, Pakistan
Country: Pakistan
Right-hand middle order batsman - Off break bowler
Test debut: 16/04/93 v West Indies - Queens Park Oval, Port of Spain

Test Career Record: *Batting & Fielding*								
Mat	Inns	N/O	Runs	H/S	Avg	100s	50s	Cat
14	23	1	757	103	34.40	1	5	4

Test Career Record: *Bowling*							
Balls	Runs	Wkts	Avg	Best	5WI	10WM	BPW
6	6	0	-	-	-	-	-

Overseas tours: WI 92/93, NZ 93/94, SL 94/95, SA 94/95, Zim 94/95, Sharjah 93/94, Pak B: Zim 90/91

Test matches: WI 92/93 (3), Zim 93/94 (3), NZ 93/94 (3), SL 94/95 (2), Aus 94/95 (2), Zim 94/95 (1)

Highest score against each country:			100s	50s
Australia	12	Karachi 94/95	0	0
New Zealand	103	Christchurch 93/94	1	2
Sri Lanka	53	Kandy 94/95	0	1
West Indies	92*	Bridgetown 92/93	0	2
Zimbabwe	40	Rawalpindi 93/94	0	0

Coopers & Lybrand world rating (batting): 57 (435)

KENNY BENJAMIN

Full name: Kenneth Charlie Griffith Benjamin
Born: 08/04/67   Liberta, Antigua
Country: West Indies
Right-arm fast bowler - Right-hand lower order batsman
Test debut: 18/04/92 v South Africa - Kensington Oval, Bridgetown

Test Career Record: *Batting & Fielding*								
Mat	Inns	N/O	Runs	H/S	Avg	100s	50s	Cat
12	15	2	88	43*	6.76	0	0	0

Test Career Record: *Bowling*							
Balls	Runs	Wkts	Avg	Best	5WI	10WM	BPW
2535	1392	47	29.61	6-66	2	0	53.93

Overseas tours: Aus 92/93, Ind 93/94, 94/95, NZ 94/95, RW: Eng 92

Test matches: SA 91/92 (1), Aus 92/93 (1), Eng 93/94 (5), Ind 94/95 (3), NZ 94/95 (2)

Best bowling against each country:			5WI	10WM
Australia	1-22	Adelaide 92/93	0	0
England	6-66	Kingston 93/94	1	0
India	5-65	Chandigarh 94/95	1	0
New Zealand	2-91	Christchurch 94/95	0	0
South Africa	2-87	Bridgetown 91/92	0	0

Coopers & Lybrand world rating (bowling): 11 (688)

WINSTON BENJAMIN

Full name: Winston Keithroy Matthew Benjamin
Born: 31/12/64   All Saints, Antigua
Country: West Indies
Right-arm fast bowler - Right-hand lower order batsman
Test debut: 25/11/87 v India - Feroz Shah Kotla, Delhi

Test Career Record: *Batting & Fielding*								
Mat	Inns	N/O	Runs	H/S	Avg	100s	50s	Cat
17	20	1	361	85	19.00	0	1	10
Test Career Record: *Bowling*								
Balls	Runs	Wkts	Avg	Best	5WI	10WM		BPW
3110	1357	52	26.09	4-46	0	0		59.80

Overseas tours: Aus 86/87, 88/89, Pak 86/87, Ind 87/88, 89/90, 93/94, Eng 88, SL 93/94, NZ 94/95, Sharjah 86/87, 88/89, 89/90, 91/92, 93/94, WC: Ind & Pak 87/88, Aus & NZ 91/92, RW: Eng 85

Test matches: Ind 87/88 (1), Pak 87/88 (3), Eng 88 (3), Ind 88/89 (1), Pak 92/93 (2), SL 93/94 (1), Eng 93/94 (5), NZ 94/95 (1)

Best bowling against each country:			5WI	10WM
England	4-52	The Oval 88	0	0
India	1-17	Delhi 87/88	0	0
New Zealand	1-94	Christchurch 94/95	0	0
Pakistan	3-30	Bridgetown 92/93	0	0
Sri Lanka	4-46	Moratuwa 93/94	0	0

Coopers & Lybrand world rating (bowling): 21 (517)

Player Profiles

MICHAEL BEVAN

Full name: Michael Gwyl Bevan
Born: 08/05/70   Belconnen, Australian Capital Territory
Country: Australia
Left-hand middle order batsman
Test debut: 28/09/94 v Pakistan - National Stadium, Karachi

Test Career Record: *Batting & Fielding*								
Mat	Inns	N/O	Runs	H/S	Avg	100s	50s	Cat
6	10	0	324	91	32.40	0	3	5

Test Career Record: *Bowling*							
Balls	Runs	Wkts	Avg	Best	5WI	10WM	BPW
90	67	1	67.00	1-21	0	0	90.00

Overseas tours: SL 94/95, Pak 94/95, Sharjah 93/94, Aus B: Zim 91/92

Test matches: Pak 94/95 (3), Eng 94/95 (3)

Highest score against each country:			100s	50s
England	35	Melbourne 94/95	0	0
Pakistan	91	Lahore 94/95	0	3

Coopers & Lybrand world rating (batting): 75= (307*)

GREG BLEWETT

Full name: Gregory Scott Blewett
Born: 29/10/71   Adelaide, South Australia
Country: Australia
Right-hand opening/middle order batsman - Right-arm medium bowler
Test debut: 26/01/95 v England - Adelaide Oval

Test Career Record: Batting & Fielding								
Mat	Inns	N/O	Runs	H/S	Avg	100s	50s	Cat
2	4	1	249	115	83.00	2	0	3
Test Career Record: Bowling								
Balls	Runs	Wkts	Avg	Best	5WI	10WM		BPW
144	91	0	-	-	-	-		-

Overseas tours: NZ 94/95, WI 94/95

Test matches: Eng 94/95 (2)

Highest score against each country:			100s	50s
England	115	Perth 94/95	2	0

Coopers & Lybrand world rating (batting): 53 (461*)

Player Profiles

DAVID BOON

Full name: David Clarence Boon MBE
Born: 29/12/60   Launceston, Tasmania, Australia
Country: Australia
Right-hand opening/middle order batsman - Right-arm medium bowler
Test debut: 23/11/84 v West Indies - Wooloongabba, Brisbane

Test Career Record: *Batting & Fielding*								
Mat	Inns	N/O	Runs	H/S	Avg	100s	50s	Cat
97	175	20	6959	200	44.89	20	30	90

Test Career Record: *Bowling*							
Balls	Runs	Wkts	Avg	Best	5WI	10WM	BPW
36	14	0	-	-	-	-	-

Overseas tours: Eng 85, 89, 93, NZ 85/86, 89/90, 92/93, 94/95, Ind 86/87, 89/90, Pak 88/89, 94/95, WI 90/91, 94/95, SL 92/93, 94/95, SA 93/94, Sharjah 85/86, 86/87, 89/90, WC: Ind & Pak 87/88, NZ 91/92

Test matches: WI 84/85 (3), Eng 85 (4), NZ 85/86 (3), Ind 85/86 (3), NZ 85/86 (3), Ind 86/87 (3), Eng 86/87 (4), NZ 87/88 (3), Eng 87/88 (1), SL 87/88 (1), Pak 88/89 (3), WI 88/89 (5), Eng 89 (6), NZ 89/90 (1), SL 89/90 (2), Pak 89/90 (2), NZ 89/90 (1), Eng 90/91 (5), WI 90/91 (5), Ind 91/92 (5), SL 92/93 (3), WI 92/93 (5), NZ 92/93 (3), Eng 93 (6), NZ 93/94 (3), SA 93/94 (3), SA 93/94 (3), Pak 94/95 (3), Eng 94/95 (5)

Highest score against each country:			100s	50s
England	184*	Sydney 87/88	7	8
India	135	Adelaide 91/92	6	2
New Zealand	200	Perth 89/90	3	8
Pakistan	114*	Karachi 94/95	1	0
South Africa	96	Cape Town 93/94	0	3
Sri Lanka	68	Colombo 92/93	0	2
West Indies	149	Sydney 88/89	3	7

Coopers & Lybrand world rating (batting): 14 (658)

Player Profiles

ALLAN BORDER

Full name: Allan Robert Border
Born: 27/07/55   Cremorne, Sydney, New South Wales, Australia
Country: Australia
Left-hand middle order batsman - Left-arm slow bowler
Test debut: 29/12/78 v England - Melbourne Cricket Ground

Test Career Record: *Batting & Fielding*

Mat	Inns	N/O	Runs	H/S	Avg	100s	50s	Cat
156	265	44	11174	205	50.56	27	63	156

Test Career Record: *Bowling*

Balls	Runs	Wkts	Avg	Best	5WI	10WM	BPW
4009	1525	39	39.10	7-46	2	1	102.79

Overseas tours: Ind 79/80, 84/85, 86/87, 89/90, Pak 79/80, 82/83, 88/89, Eng 80, 81, 85, 89, 93, SL 80/81, 82/83, 92/93, NZ 81/82, 85/86, 89/90, 92/93, WI 83/84, 90/91, 92/93, SA 93/94, Sharjah 84/85, 86/87, 89/90, WC: Eng 79, 83, Ind & Pak 87/88, NZ 91/92, RW: Eng 87

Test matches: Eng 78/79 (3), Pak 78/79 (2), Ind 79/80 (6), WI 79/80 (3), Eng 79/80 (3), Pak 79/80 (3), Eng 80 (1), NZ 80/81 (3), Ind 80/81 (3), Eng 81 (6), Pak 81/82 (3), WI 81/82 (3), NZ 81/82 (3), Pak 82/83 (3), Eng 82/83 (5), SL 82/83 (1), Pak 83/84 (5), WI 83/84 (5), WI 84/85 (5), Eng 85 (6), NZ 85/86 (3), Ind 85/86 (3), NZ 85/86 (3), Ind 86/87 (3), Eng 86/87 (5), NZ 87/88 (3), Eng 87/88 (1), SL 87/88 (1), Pak 88/89 (3), WI 88/89 (5), Eng 89 (6), NZ 89/90 (1), SL 89/90 (2), Pak 89/90 (3), NZ 89/90 (1), Eng 90/91 (5), WI 90/91 (5), Ind 91/92 (5), SL 92/93

(3), WI 92/93 (5), NZ 92/93 (3), Eng 93 (6), NZ 93/94 (3), SA 93/94 (3), SA 93/94 (3)

Highest score against each country:			100s	50s
England	200*	Headingley 93	8	21
India	163	Melbourne 85/86	4	9
New Zealand	205	Adelaide 87/88	5	6
Pakistan	153	Lahore 79/80	6	8
South Africa	84	Adelaide 93/94	0	1
Sri Lanka	106	Moratuwa 92/93	1	4
West Indies	126	Adelaide 81/82	3	14

Player Profiles

DAVID BRAIN

Full name: David Hayden Brain
Born: 04/10/64   Salisbury (Harare), Zimbabwe
Country: Zimbabwe
Left-arm medium bowler - Right-hand lower order batsman
Test debut: 07/11/92 v New Zealand - Harare Sports Club

Test Career Record: *Batting & Fielding*								
Mat	Inns	N/O	Runs	H/S	Avg	100s	50s	Cat
9	13	2	115	28	10.45	0	0	1

Test Career Record: *Bowling*							
Balls	Runs	Wkts	Avg	Best	5WI	10WM	BPW
1810	915	30	30.50	5-42	1	0	60.33

Overseas tours: Ind 92/93, 93/94, Eng 93, Pak 93/94, Aus 94/95, Sharjah 92/93

Test matches: NZ 92/93 (1), Ind 92/93 (1), Pak 93/94 (2), SL 94/95 (2), Pak 94/95 (3)

Best bowling against each country:			5WI	10WM
India	2-146	Delhi 92/93	0	0
New Zealand	3-49	Harare 92/93	0	0
Pakistan	5-42	Lahore 93/94	1	0
Sri Lanka	2-48	Harare 94/95	0	0

Coopers & Lybrand world rating (bowling): 33 (367*)

ALISTAIR CAMPBELL

Full name: Alistair Douglas Ross Campbell
Born: 23/09/72   Salisbury (Harare), Zimbabwe
Country: Zimbabwe
Left-hand middle order batsman - Off break bowler
Test debut: 18/10/92 v India - Harare Sports Club

\multicolumn{9}{l}{Test Career Record: *Batting & Fielding*}

Test Career Record: *Batting & Fielding*
Mat	Inns	N/O	Runs	H/S	Avg	100s	50s	Cat
13	21	1	732	99	36.60	0	7	9

Test Career Record: *Bowling*
Balls	Runs	Wkts	Avg	Best	5WI	10WM	BPW
18	4	0	-	-	-	-	-

Overseas tours: Ind 92/93, 93/94, Eng 93, Pak 93/94, Aus 94/95, Sharjah 92/93, WC: Aus & NZ 91/92

Test matches: Ind 92/93 (1), NZ 92/93 (2), Ind 92/93 (1), Pak 93/94 (3), SL 94/95 (3), Pak 94/95 (3)

Highest score against each country:			100s	50s
India	61	Delhi 92/93	0	1
New Zealand	52	Harare 92/93	0	1
Pakistan	75	Rawalpindi 93/94	0	4
Sri Lanka	99	Harare 94/95	0	1

Coopers & Lybrand world rating (batting): 31= (563)

SHIVNARINE CHANDERPAUL

Full name: Shivnarine Chanderpaul
Born: 18/08/74   Unity Village, Guyana
Country: West Indies
Left-hand middle order batsman - Leg break bowler
Test debut: 17/03/94 v England - Bourda, Georgetown

\multicolumn{9}{l}{**Test Career Record:** *Batting & Fielding*}
Mat	Inns	N/O	Runs	H/S	Avg	100s	50s	Cat
7	10	3	433	77	61.85	0	6	4

Test Career Record: *Bowling*							
Balls	Runs	Wkts	Avg	Best	5WI	10WM	BPW
540	282	2	141.00	1-63	0	0	270.00

Overseas tours: Ind 94/95, NZ 94/95, WI under 19: Eng 93

Test matches: Eng 93/94 (4), Ind 94/95 (1), NZ 94/95 (2)

Highest score against each country:			100s	50s
England	77	Bridgetown 93/94	0	4
India	11*	Nagpur 94/95	0	0
New Zealand	69	Christchurch 94/95	0	2

Coopers & Lybrand world rating (batting): 58= (429*)

RAJESH CHAUHAN

Full name: Rajesh Kumar Chauhan
Born: 19/12/66   Ranchi, India
Country: India
Off break bowler - Right-hand lower order batsman
Test debut: 29/01/93 v England - Eden Gardens, Calcutta

Test Career Record: *Batting & Fielding*								
Mat	Inns	N/O	Runs	H/S	Avg	100s	50s	Cat
13	10	3	64	15*	9.14	0	0	8
Test Career Record: *Bowling*								
Balls	Runs	Wkts	Avg	Best	5WI	10WM		BPW
3131	1151	33	34.87	3-8	0	0		94.87

Overseas tours: SL 93/94, 94/95, NZ 93/94, Sharjah 93/94

Test matches: Eng 92/93 (3), Zim 92/93 (1), SL 93/94 (3), SL 93/94 (3), NZ 93/94 (1), WI 94/95 (2)

Best bowling against each country:			5WI	10WM
England	3-30	Calcutta 92/93	0	0
New Zealand	3-97	Hamilton 93/94	0	0
Sri Lanka	3-8	Ahmedabad 93/94	0	0
West Indies	1-45	Bombay 94/95	0	0
Zimbabwe	2-68	Delhi 92/93	0	0

Coopers & Lybrand world rating (bowling): 36 (357*)

Player Profiles

JOHN CRAWLEY

Full name: John Paul Crawley
Born: 21/09/71   Maldon, Essex, England
Country: England
Right-hand middle order batsman - Right-arm medium bowler
Test debut: 21/07/94 v South Africa - Lord's, London

Test Career Record: *Batting & Fielding*								
Mat	Inns	N/O	Runs	H/S	Avg	100s	50s	Cat
6	10	0	230	72	23.00	0	2	5

Overseas tours: Aus 94/95, Eng A: SA 93/94, Young Eng: Aus 89/90, NZ 90/91

Test matches: SA 94 (3), Aus 94/95 (3)

Highest score against each country:			100s	50s
Australia	72	Sydney 94/95	0	2
South Africa	38	Headingley 94	0	0

Coopers & Lybrand world rating (batting): 74 (308*)

'HANSIE' CRONJE

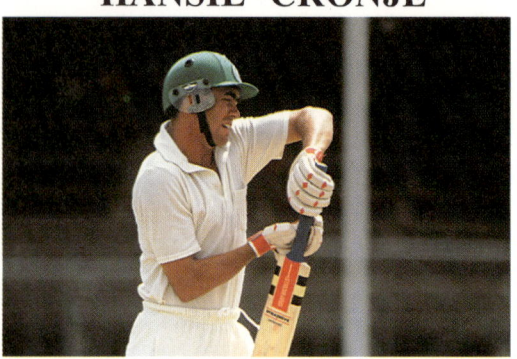

Full name: Wessel Johannes Cronje
Born: 25/09/69 Bloemfontein, South Africa
Country: South Africa
Right-hand middle order batsman - Right-arm medium bowler
Test debut: 18/04/92 v West Indies - Kensington Oval, Bridgetown

Test Career Record: *Batting & Fielding*								
Mat	Inns	N/O	Runs	H/S	Avg	100s	50s	Cat
20	36	4	1200	135	37.50	4	3	9

Test Career Record: *Bowling*							
Balls	Runs	Wkts	Avg	Best	5WI	10WM	BPW
1417	427	6	71.16	2-17	0	0	236.16

Overseas tours: WI 91/92, SL 93/94, Ind 93/94, Aus 93/94, Eng 94, Pak 94/95, NZ 94/95, WC: Aus & NZ 91/92

Test matches: WI 91/92 (1), Ind 92/93 (3), SL 93/94 (3), Aus 93/94 (3), Aus 93/94 (3), Eng 94 (3), NZ 93/94 (3), Pak 94/95 (1)

Highest score against each country:			100s	50s
Australia	122	Johannesburg 93/94	1	1
England	38	The Oval 94	0	0
India	135	Port Elizabeth 92/93	1	0
New Zealand	112	Cape Town 94/95	1	1
Pakistan	48	Johannesburg 94/95	0	0
Sri Lanka	122	Colombo 93/94	1	1
West Indies	5	Bridgetown 91/92	0	0

Coopers & Lybrand world rating (batting): 18 (625)

MARTIN CROWE

Full name: Martin David Crowe MBE
Born: 22/09/62   Henderson, Auckland, New Zealand
Country: New Zealand
Right-hand middle order batsman - Right-arm medium bowler
Test debut: 26/02/82 v Australia - Basin Reserve, Wellington

Test Career Record: *Batting & Fielding*

Mat	Inns	N/O	Runs	H/S	Avg	100s	50s	Cat
73	126	11	5364	299	46.64	17	18	69

Test Career Record: *Bowling*

Balls	Runs	Wkts	Avg	Best	5WI	10WM	BPW
1383	678	14	48.42	2-25	0	0	98.78

Overseas tours: Aus 82/83, 84/85, 85/86, 87/88, 89/90, 90/91, 93/94, Eng 83, 86, 90, 94, SL 83/84, 84/85, 85/86, 86/87, 92/93, Pak 84/85, 90/91, WI 84/85, Zim 92/93, SA 94/95, Sharjah 85/86, 89/90, WC: Ind 87/88, RW: Eng 85, 89

Test matches: Aus 81/82 (3), Eng 83 (4), Eng 83/84 (3), SL 83/84 (3), Pak 84/85 (3), Pak 84/85 (3), WI 84/85 (4), Aus 85/86 (3), Aus 85/86 (3), Eng 86 (3), WI 86/87 (3), SL 86/87 (1), Aus 87/88 (3), Eng 87/88 (3), Pak 88/89 (2), Aus 89/90 (1), Ind 89/90 (3), Eng 90 (3), Pak 90/91 (3), SL 90/91 (2), Eng 91/92 (3), Zim 92/93 (2), SL 92/93 (2), Aus 92/93 (3), Aus 93/94 (1), Eng 94 (3), SA 94/95 (3)

Highest score against each country:			100s	50s
Australia	188	Brisbane 85/86	3	6
England	143	Wellington 87/88	5	3
India	113	Auckland 89/90	1	0
Pakistan	174	Wellington 88/89	2	6
South Africa	83	Johannesburg 94/95	0	1
Sri Lanka	299	Wellington 90/91	2	0
West Indies	188	Georgetown 84/85	3	1
Zimbabwe	140	Harare 92/93	1	1

Coopers & Lybrand world rating (batting): 23= (603)

Player Profiles

DARYLL CULLINAN

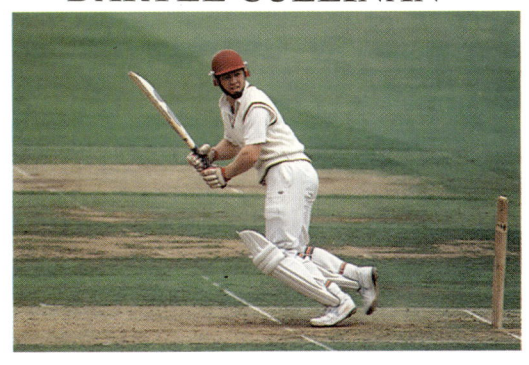

Full name: Daryll John Cullinan
Born: 04/03/67 Kimberley, South Africa
Country: South Africa
Right-hand middle order batsman - Off break bowler
Test debut: 02/01/93 v India - Newlands, Cape Town

Test Career Record: *Batting & Fielding*								
Mat	Inns	N/O	Runs	H/S	Avg	100s	50s	Cat
12	22	2	669	102	33.45	1	4	4

Overseas tours: SL 93/94, Ind 93/94, Aus 93/94, Eng 94, Pak 94/95, NZ 94/95

Test matches: Ind 92/93 (1), SL 93/94 (3), Aus 93/94 (3), Eng 94 (1), NZ 94/95 (3), Pak 94/95 (1)

Highest score against each country:			100s	50s
Australia	10	Adelaide 93/94	0	0
England	94	The Oval 94	0	1
India	46	Cape Town 92/93	0	0
New Zealand	58	Johannesburg 94/95	0	1
Pakistan	69 *	Johannesburg 94/95	0	1
Sri Lanka	102	Colombo 93/94	1	1

Coopers & Lybrand world rating (batting): 46= (504)

ARAVINDA DE SILVA

Full name: Pinnaduwage Aravinda De Silva
Born: 17/10/65 Colombo, Sri Lanka
Country: Sri Lanka
Right-hand middle order batsman - Off break bowler
Test debut: 23/08/84 v England - Lord's, London

Test Career Record: *Batting & Fielding*

Mat	Inns	N/O	Runs	H/S	Avg	100s	50s	Cat
46	79	4	2872	267	38.29	7	12	21

Test Career Record: *Bowling*

Balls	Runs	Wkts	Avg	Best	5WI	10WM	BPW
780	413	11	37.54	3-39	0	0	70.90

Overseas tours: Eng 84, 88, 90, 91, Aus 84/85, 87/88, 89/90, Pak 85/86, 91/92, Ind 86/87, 89/90, 90/91, 93/94, NZ 90/91, Zim 94/95, SA 94/95, Ban 88/89, Sharjah 83/84, 85/86, 86/87, 87/88, 88/89, 89/90, 90/91, 92/93, 93/94, WC: Ind & Pak 87/88, Aus & NZ 91/92

Test matches: Eng 84 (1), Ind 85/86 (3), Pak 85/86 (3), Pak 85/86 (3), Ind 86/87 (3), Aus 87/88 (1), Eng 88 (1), Aus 89/90 (2), Ind 90/91 (1), NZ 90/91 (3), Eng 91 (1), Pak 91/92 (3), Aus 92/93 (3), NZ 92/93 (2), Eng 92/93 (1), Ind 93/94 (3), SA 93/94 (3), WI 93/94 (1), Ind 93/94 (3), Pak 94/95 (2), Zim 94/95 (3)

Highest score against each country:			100s	50s
Australia	167	Brisbane 89/90	1	4
England	80	Colombo 92/93	0	1
India	148	Colombo 93/94	1	2
New Zealand	267	Wellington 90/91	2	2
Pakistan	127	Colombo 94/95	3	0
South Africa	82	Colombo 93/94	0	2
West Indies	53	Moratuwa 93/94	0	1
Zimbabwe	41 *	Harare 94/95	0	0

Coopers & Lybrand world rating (batting): 36 (544)

Player Profiles

'FANIE' DE VILLIERS

Full name: Petrus Stephanus de Villiers
Born: 13/10/64   Vereeniging, Transvaal, South Africa
Country: South Africa
Right-arm fast bowler - Right-hand lower order batsman
Test debut: 26/12/93 v Australia - Melbourne Cricket Ground

Test Career Record: *Batting & Fielding*								
Mat	*Inns*	*N/O*	*Runs*	*H/S*	*Avg*	*100s*	*50s*	*Cat*
13	18	5	218	66*	16.76	0	1	8
Test Career Record: *Bowling*								
Balls	*Runs*	*Wkts*	*Avg*	*Best*	*5WI*	*10WM*		*BPW*
3685	1613	64	25.20	6-43	4	2		57.57

Overseas tours: SL 93/94, Aus 93/94, Eng 94, Pak 94/95, NZ 94/95

Test matches: Aus 93/94 (3), Aus 93/94 (3), Eng 94 (3), NZ 94/95 (3), Pak 94/95 (1)

Best bowling against each country:			5WI	10WM
Australia	6-43	Sydney 93/94	1	1
England	4-62	The Oval 94	0	0
New Zealand	5-61	Cape Town 94/95	2	0
Pakistan	6-81	Johannesburg 94/95	1	1

Coopers & Lybrand world rating (bowling): 5 (803)

PHILLIP DEFREITAS

Full name: Phillip Anthony Jason DeFreitas
Born: 18/02/66 Scotts Head, Dominica
Country: England
Right-arm fast medium bowler - Right-hand middle order batsman
Test debut: 14/11/86 v Australia - Woolloongabba, Brisbane

Test Career Record: Batting & Fielding								
Mat	Inns	N/O	Runs	H/S	Avg	100s	50s	Cat
43	66	5	910	88	14.91	0	4	14

Test Career Record: Bowling							
Balls	Runs	Wkts	Avg	Best	5WI	10WM	BPW
9676	4585	138	33.22	7-70	4	0	70.11

Overseas tours: Aus 86/87, 87/88, 90/91, 94/95, NZ 87/88, 90/91, 91/92, Pak 87/88, Ind 89/90, 92/93, WI 89/90, SL 92/93, Sharjah 86/87, WC: Ind & Pak 87/88, Aus & NZ 91/92

Test matches: Aus 86/87 (4), Pak 87 (1), Pak 87/88 (2), NZ 87/88 (2), WI 88 (3), Aus 89 (1), WI 89/90 (2), NZ 90 (2), Aus 90/91 (3), WI 91 (5), SL 91 (1), NZ 91/92 (3), Pak 92 (2), Ind 92/93 (1), Aus 93 (1), NZ 94 (3), SA 94 (3), Aus 94/95 (4)

Best bowling against each country:			5WI	10WM
Australia	4-56	Adelaide 90/91	0	0
India	0-75	Bombay 92/93	0	0
New Zealand	5-53	Trent Bridge 90	2	0
Pakistan	5-86	Karachi 87/88	1	0
South Africa	4-89	Headingley 94	0	0
Sri Lanka	7-70	Lord's 91	1	0
West Indies	4-34	Headingley 91	0	0

Coopers & Lybrand world rating (bowling): 17 (553)

Player Profiles

ALLAN DONALD

Full name: Allan Anthony Donald
Born: 20/10/66   Bloemfontein, South Africa
Country: South Africa
Right-arm fast bowler - Right-hand lower order batsman
Test debut: 18/04/92 v West Indies - Kensington Oval, Bridgetown

Test Career Record: *Batting & Fielding*								
Mat	*Inns*	*N/O*	*Runs*	*H/S*	*Avg*	*100s*	*50s*	*Cat*
18	24	13	128	27	11.63	0	0	5

Test Career Record: *Bowling*							
Balls	*Runs*	*Wkts*	*Avg*	*Best*	*5WI*	*10WM*	*BPW*
4193	2094	79	26.50	7-84	4	1	53.07

Overseas tours: Ind 91/92, 93/94, WI 91/92, SL 93/94, Aus 93/94, Eng 94, NZ 94/95, WC: Aus & NZ 91/92

Test matches: WI 91/92 (1), Ind 92/93 (4), SL 93/94 (3), Aus 93/94 (3), Aus 93/94 (3), Eng 94 (3), Pak 94/95 (1)

Best bowling against each country:			5WI	10WM
Australia	4-83	Sydney 93/94	0	0
England	5-74	Lord's 94	1	0
India	7-84	Port Elizabeth 92/93	2	1
Pakistan	2-53	Johannesburg 94/95	0	0
Sri Lanka	5-69	Moratuwa 93/94	1	0
West Indies	4-77	Bridgetown 91/92	0	0

Coopers & Lybrand world rating (bowling): 12 (686)

SIMON DOULL

Full name: Simon Blair Doull
Born: 06/08/69   Pukekohe, New Zealand
Country: New Zealand
Right-arm fast medium bowler - Right-hand lower order batsman
Test debut: 01/11/92 v Zimbabwe - Bulawayo Athletic Club

Test Career Record: *Batting & Fielding*								
Mat	Inns	N/O	Runs	H/S	Avg	100s	50s	Cat
11	18	2	210	31*	13.12	0	0	8
Test Career Record: *Bowling*								
Balls	Runs	Wkts	Avg	Best	5WI	10WM		BPW
2012	1077	33	32.63	5-66	2	0		60.96

Overseas tours: Zim 92/93, Aus 93/94, Ind 94/95, SA 94/95

Test matches: Zim 92/93 (1), Aus 93/94 (2), Pak 93/94 (3), SA 94/95 (3), WI 94/95 (2)

Best bowling against each country:			5WI	10WM
Australia	2-105	Brisbane 93/94	0	0
Pakistan	5-66	Auckland 93/94	1	0
South Africa	5-73	Durban 94/95	1	0
West Indies	2-162	Wellington 94/95	0	0
Zimbabwe	1-29	Bulawayo 92/93	0	0

Coopers & Lybrand world rating (bowling): 25 (453*)

Player Profiles

DAMIEN FLEMING

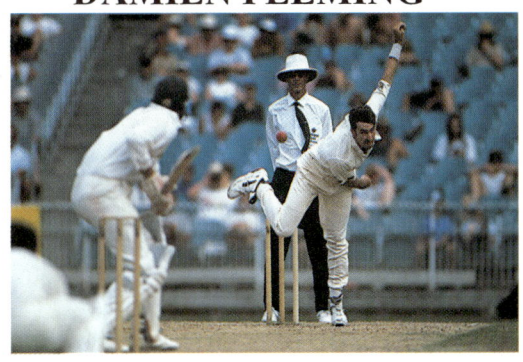

Full name: Damien William Fleming
Born: 24/04/70   Bentleigh, Victoria, Australia
Country: Australia
Right-arm fast bowler - Right-hand lower order batsman
Test debut: 05/10/94 v Pakistan - Rawalpindi Stadium

Test Career Record: *Batting & Fielding*								
Mat	Inns	N/O	Runs	H/S	Avg	100s	50s	Cat
4	4	0	40	24	10.00	0	0	2

Test Career Record: *Bowling*							
Balls	Runs	Wkts	Avg	Best	5WI	10WM	BPW
902	435	17	25.58	4-75	0	0	53.05

Overseas tours: SL 94/95, Pak 94/95, WI 94/95, Sharjah 93/94

Test matches: Pak 94/95 (1), Eng 94/95 (3)

Best bowling against each country:			5WI	10WM
England	3-52	Sydney 94/95	0	0
Pakistan	4-75	Rawalpindi 94/95	0	0

Coopers & Lybrand world rating (bowling): 31 (398*)

STEPHEN FLEMING

Full name: Stephen Paul Fleming
Born: 01/04/73   Christchurch, New Zealand
Country: New Zealand
Left-hand middle order batsman - Right-arm medium bowler
Test debut: 19/03/94 v India - Trust Bank Park, Hamilton

Test Career Record: *Batting & Fielding*								
Mat	Inns	N/O	Runs	H/S	Avg	100s	50s	Cat
9	17	0	641	92	37.70	0	5	6

Overseas tours: Eng 94, Ind 94/95, SA 94/95, Sharjah 93/94

Test matches: Ind 93/94 (1), Eng 94 (3), SA 94/95 (3), WI 94/95 (2)

Highest score against each country:			100s	50s
England	54	Trent Bridge 94	0	1
India	92	Hamilton 93/94	0	1
South Africa	79	Cape Town 94/95	0	2
West Indies	56	Christchurch 94/95	0	1

Coopers & Lybrand world rating (batting): 35 (546*)

Player Profiles

ANDREW FLOWER

Full name: Andrew Flower
Born: 28/04/68   Cape Town, South Africa
Country: Zimbabwe
Left-hand middle order batsman - Wicket-Keeper
Test debut: 18/10/92 v India - Harare Sports Club

Test Career Record: *Batting & Fielding*									
Mat	*Inns*	*N/O*	*Runs*	*H/S*	*Avg*	*100s*	*50s*	*Cat*	*St*
13	20	3	835	156	49.11	2	6	29	2

Test Career Record: *Bowling*							
Balls	*Runs*	*Wkts*	*Avg*	*Best*	*5WI*	*10WM*	*BPW*
1	0	0	-	-	-	-	-

Overseas tours: Ind 92/93, 93/94, Eng 93, Pak 93/94, Aus 94/95, Sharjah 92/93, WC: Aus & NZ 91/92

Test matches: Ind 92/93 (1), NZ 92/93 (2), Ind 92/93 (1), Pak 93/94 (3), SL 94/95 (3), Pak 94/95 (3)

Highest score against each country:			100s	50s
India	115	Delhi 92/93	1	2
New Zealand	81	Bulawayo 92/93	0	1
Pakistan	156	Harare 94/95	1	2
Sri Lanka	50	Bulawayo 94/95	0	1

Coopers & Lybrand world rating (batting): 17 (636)

GRANT FLOWER

Full name: Grant William Flower
Born: 20/12/70   Salisbury (Harare), Zimbabwe
Country: Zimbabwe
Right-hand middle order batsman - Left-arm slow bowler
Test debut: 18/10/92 v India   Harare Sports Club

Test Career Record: *Batting & Fielding*								
Mat	Inns	N/O	Runs	H/S	Avg	100s	50s	Cat
13	21	1	627	201*	31.35	1	2	6
Test Career Record: *Bowling*								
Balls	Runs	Wkts	Avg	Best	5WI	10WM		BPW
366	173	2	86.50	1-8	0	0		183.00

Overseas tours: Eng 90, 93, Ind 92/93, 93/94, Pak 93/94, Sharjah 92/93

Test matches: Ind 92/93 (1), NZ 92/93 (2), Ind 92/93 (1), Pak 93/94 (3), SL 94/95 (3), Pak 94/95 (3)

Highest score against each country:			100s	50s
India	96	Delhi 92/93	0	2
New Zealand	45	Bulawayo 92/93	0	0
Pakistan	201*	Harare 94/95	1	0
Sri Lanka	41	Harare 94/95	0	0

Coopers & Lybrand world rating (batting): 58= (429)

Player Profiles

ANGUS FRASER

Full name: Angus Robert Charles Fraser
Born: 08/08/65   Billinge, Lancashire, England
Country: England
Right-arm fast medium bowler - Right-hand lower order batsman
Test debut: 06/07/89 v Australia - Edgbaston, Birmingham

Test Career Record: *Batting & Fielding*								
Mat	Inns	N/O	Runs	H/S	Avg	100s	50s	Cat
24	34	4	233	29	7.76	0	0	6

Test Career Record: *Bowling*							
Balls	Runs	Wkts	Avg	Best	5WI	10WM	BPW
6444	2759	99	27.86	8-76	7	0	65.09

Overseas tours: Ind 89/90, WI 89/90, 93/94, Aus 90/91, 94/95, NZ 90/91

Test matches: Aus 89 (3), WI 89/90 (2), Ind 90 (3), Aus 90/91 (3), Aus 93 (1), WI 93/94 (4), NZ 94 (3), SA 94 (2), Aus 94/95 (3)

Best bowling against each country:			5WI	10WM
Australia	6-82	Melbourne 90/91	3	0
India	5-104	Lord's 90	2	0
New Zealand	2-40	Trent Bridge 94	0	0
South Africa	3-72	Lord's 94	0	0
West Indies	8-75	Bridgetown 93/94	2	0

Coopers & Lybrand world rating (bowling): 14 (639)

MIKE GATTING

Full name: Michael William Gatting OBE
Born: 06/06/57   Kingsbury, Middlesex, England
Country: England
Right-hand middle order batsman - Right-arm medium bowler
Test debut: 18/01/78 v Pakistan - National Stadium, Karachi

Test Career Record: *Batting & Fielding*

Mat	Inns	N/O	Runs	H/S	Avg	100s	50s	Cat
79	138	14	4409	207	35.55	10	21	59

Test Career Record: *Bowling*

Balls	Runs	Wkts	Avg	Best	5WI	10WM	BPW
752	317	4	79.25	1-14	0	0	188.00

Overseas tours: Pak 77/78, 83/84, 87/88, NZ 77/78, 83/84, 87/88, WI 80/81, 85/86, Ind 81/82, 84/85, 92/93, SL 81/82, 84/85, 92/93, Aus 84/85, 86/87, 87/88, 94/95, WC: Ind & Pak 87/88

Test matches: Pak 77/78 (1), NZ 77/78 (1), WI 80 (4), Aus 80 (1), WI 80/81 (1), Aus 81 (6), Ind 81/82 (5), Pak 82 (3), NZ 83 (2), NZ 83/84 (2), Pak 83/84 (3), WI 84 (1), Ind 84/85 (5), Aus 85 (6), WI 85/86 (1), Ind 86 (3), NZ 86 (3), Aus 86/87 (5), Pak 87 (5), Pak 87/88 (3), Aus 87/88 (1), NZ 87/88 (3), WI 88 (2), Aus 89 (1), Ind 92/93 (3), SL 92/93 (1), Aus 93 (2), Aus 94/95 (5)

Highest score against each country:			100s	50s
Australia	160	Old Trafford 85	4	12
India	207	Madras 84/85	3	3
New Zealand	121	The Oval 86	1	1
Pakistan	150*	The Oval 87	2	4
Sri Lanka	29	Colombo 92/93	0	0
West Indies	56	Old Trafford 80	0	1

Coopers & Lybrand world rating (batting): 71 (345)

GRAHAM GOOCH

Full name: Graham Alan Gooch OBE
Born: 23/07/53   Whipps Cross, Leytonstone, Essex, England
Country: England
Right-hand opening batsman   Right arm medium bowler
Test debut: 10/07/75 v Australia - Edgbaston, Birmingham

Test Career Record: *Batting & Fielding*

Mat	Inns	N/O	Runs	H/S	Avg	100s	50s	Cat
118	215	6	8900	333	42.58	20	46	103

Test Career Record: *Bowling*

Balls	Runs	Wkts	Avg	Best	5WI	10WM	BPW
2655	1069	23	46.47	3-39	0	0	115.43

Overseas tours: Aus 78/79, 79/80, 90/91, 94/95, Ind 79/80, 81/82, 89/90, 92/93, WI 80/81, 85/86, 89/90, SL 81/82, Pak 87/88, NZ 90/91, 91/92, WC: Ind & Pak 87/88, Aus & NZ 91/92

Test matches: Aus 75 (2), Pak 78 (2), NZ 78 (3), Aus 78/79 (6), Ind 79 (4), Aus 79/80 (2), Ind 79/80 (1), WI 80 (5), Aus 80 (1), WI 80/81 (4), Aus 81 (5), Ind 81/82 (6), SL 81/82 (1), Aus 85 (6), WI 85/86 (5), Ind 86 (3), NZ 86 (3), Pak 87/88 (3), WI 88 (5), SL 88 (1), Aus 89 (5), WI 89/90 (2), NZ 90 (3), Ind 90 (3), Aus 90/91 (4), WI 91 (5), SL 91 (1), NZ 91/92 (3), Pak 92 (5), Ind 92/93 (2), Aus 93 (6), NZ 94 (3), SA 94 (3), Aus 94/95 (5)

Highest score against each country:			100s	50s
Australia	196	The Oval 85	4	16
India	333	Lord's 90	5	8
New Zealand	210	Trent Bridge 94	4	3
Pakistan	135	Headingley 92	1	5
South Africa	33	The Oval 94	0	0
Sri Lanka	174	Lord's 91	1	1
West Indies	154*	Headingley 91	5	13

Coopers & Lybrand world rating (batting): 22 (606)

DARREN GOUGH

Full name: Darren Gough
Born: 18/09/70   Barnsley, Yorkshire, England
Country: England
Right-arm fast bowler - Right-hand middle order batsman
Test debut: 30/06/94 v New Zealand   Old Trafford, Manchester

Test Career Record: *Batting & Fielding*								
Mat	Inns	N/O	Runs	H/S	Avg	100s	50s	Cat
7	10	3	244	65	34.85	0	2	4
Test Career Record: *Bowling*								
Balls	Runs	Wkts	Avg	Best	5WI	10WM		BPW
1939	991	37	26.78	6-49	1	0		52.40

Overseas tours: Aus 94/95, Eng A: SA 93/94, Young Eng: Aus 89/90

Test matches: NZ 94 (1), SA 94 (3), Aus 94/95 (3)

Best bowling against each country:			5WI	10WM
Australia	6-49	Sydney 94/95	1	0
New Zealand	4-47	Old Trafford 94	0	0
South Africa	4-46	Lord's 94	0	0

Coopers & Lybrand world rating (bowling): 15 (588*)

Player Profiles

ASANKA GURUSINHA

Full name: Asanka Pradeep Gurusinha
Born: 16/09/66   Colombo, Sri Lanka
Country: Sri Lanka
Left-hand middle order batsman - Right-arm medium bowler - Wicket-Keeper
Test debut: 07/11/85 v Pakistan - National Stadium, Karachi

Test Career Record: *Batting & Fielding*								
Mat	Inns	N/O	Runs	H/S	Avg	100s	50s	Cat
31	52	7	1787	137	39.71	5	6	22
Test Career Record: *Bowling*								
Balls	Runs	Wkts	Avg	Best	5WI	10WM	BPW	
1210	593	18	32.94	2-7	0	0	67.22	

Overseas tours: Pak 85/86, 91/92, Ind 86/87, 89/90, 90/91, Aus 87/88, 89/90, Eng 90, 91, NZ 90/91, Zim 94/95, SA 94/95, Sharjah 85/86, 86/87, 87/88, 89/90, 90/91, 92/93, 93/94, WC: Ind & Pak 87/88, Aus & NZ 91/92

Test matches: Pak 85/86 (1), Pak 85/86 (2), Ind 86/87 (3), NZ 86/87 (1), Aus 89/90 (2), Ind 90/91 (1), NZ 90/91 (3), Eng 91 (1), Pak 91/92 (3), Aus 92/93 (3), NZ 92/93 (2), Eng 92/93 (1), Ind 93/94 (3), SA 93/94 (1), Pak 94/95 (1), Zim 94/95 (3)

Highest score against each country:			100s	50s
Australia	137	Colombo 92/93	1	0
England	43	Colombo 92/93	0	0
India	56	Colombo 93/94	0	2
New Zealand	119	Hamilton 90/91	2	2
Pakistan	116*	Colombo 85/86	1	0
South Africa	27	Moratuwa 93/94	0	0
Zimbabwe	128	Harare 94/95	1	2

Coopers & Lybrand world rating (batting): 52 (469)

MATTHEW HART

Full name: Matthew Norman Hart
Born: 16/05/72   Hamilton, New Zealand
Country: New Zealand
Left-arm slow bowler - Left-hand lower order batsman
Test debut: 17/02/94 v Pakistan - Basin Reserve, Wellington

Test Career Record: *Batting & Fielding*								
Mat	Inns	N/O	Runs	H/S	Avg	100s	50s	Cat
11	19	3	283	45	17.68	0	0	5

Test Career Record: *Bowling*							
Balls	Runs	Wkts	Avg	Best	5WI	10WM	BPW
2817	1251	26	48.11	5-77	1	0	108.34

Overseas tours: Eng 94, Ind 94/95, SA 94/95, Sharjah 93/94

Test matches: Pak 93/94 (2), Ind 93/94 (1), Eng 94 (3), SA 94/95 (3), WI 94/95 (2)

Best bowling against each country:			5WI	10WM
England	1-50	Lord's 94	0	0
	1-50	Old Trafford 94		
India	2-66	Hamilton 93/94	0	0
Pakistan	3-47	Christchurch 93/94	0	0
South Africa	5-77	Johannesburg 94/95	1	0
West Indies	0-75	Christchurch 94/95	0	0

Coopers & Lybrand world rating (bowling): 64 (196*)

Player Profiles

DESMOND HAYNES

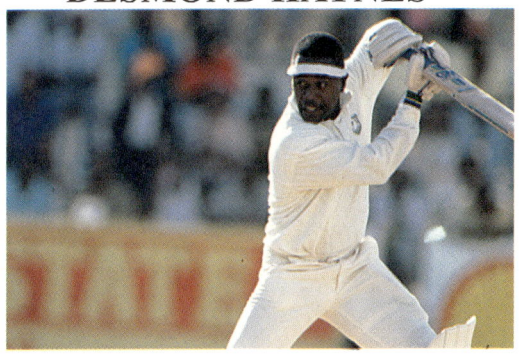

Full name: Desmond Leo Haynes
Born: 15/02/56 Holders Hill, St James, Barbados
Country: West Indies
Right-hand opening batsman - Leg break & googly bowler
Test debut: 03/03/78 v Australia - Queens Park Oval, Port of Spain

Test Career Record: *Batting & Fielding*								
Mat	*Inns*	*N/O*	*Runs*	*H/S*	*Avg*	*100s*	*50s*	*Cat*
116	202	25	7487	184	42.29	18	39	65

Test Career Record: *Bowling*							
Balls	*Runs*	*Wkts*	*Avg*	*Best*	*5WI*	*10WM*	*BPW*
18	8	1	8.00	1-2	0	0	18.00

Overseas tours: Aus 79/80, 81/82, 83/84, 84/85, 86/87, 88/89, 91/92, 92/93, NZ 79/80, 86/87, Eng 80, 84, 88, 91, Pak 80/81, 85/86, 86/87, 90/91, 91/92, Ind 83/84, 87/88, 89/90, 93/94, SA 92/93, SL 93/94, Sharjah 85/86, 86/87, 88/89, 89/90, 93/94, WC: Eng 79, 83, Ind & Pak 86/87, Aus & NZ 91/92, Young WI: Zim 81/82, RW: Eng 87

Test matches: Aus 77/78 (2), Aus 79/80 (3), NZ 79/80 (3), Eng 80 (5), Pak 80/81 (4), Eng 80/81 (4), Aus 81/82 (3), Ind 82/83 (5), Ind 83/84 (6), Aus 83/84 (5), Eng 84 (5), Aus 84/85 (5), NZ 84/85 (4), Eng 85/86 (5), Pak 86/87 (3), NZ 86/87 (3), Ind 87/88 (4), Pak 87/88 (3), Eng 88 (4), Aus 88/89 (5), Ind 88/89 (4), Eng 89/90 (4), Pak 90/91 (3), Aus 90/91 (5), Eng 91 (5), SA 91/92 (1), Aus 92/93 (5), Pak 92/93 (3), SL 93/94 (1), Eng 93/94 (4)

Highest score against each country:			100s	50s
Australia	145	Bridgetown 83/84	5	14
England	184	Lord's 80	5	13
India	136	St John's 82/83	2	4
New Zealand	122	Christchurch 79/80	3	5
Pakistan	143 *	Port of Spain 92/93	3	2
South Africa	58	Bridgetown 91/92	0	1
Sri Lanka	20	Moratuwa 93/94	0	0

Coopers & Lybrand world rating (batting): 9 (698)

Player Profiles

IAN HEALY

Full name: Ian Andrew Healy
Born: 30/04/64   Spring Hill, Brisbane, Queensland, Australia
Country: Australia
Right-hand middle order batsman - Wicket-Keeper
Test debut: 15/09/88 v Pakistan - National Stadium, Karachi

Test Career Record: *Batting & Fielding*									
Mat	Inns	N/O	Runs	H/S	Avg	100s	50s	Cat	St
69	103	13	2429	113*	26.98	2	15	222	16

Overseas tours: Pak 88/89, 94/95, Eng 89, 93, NZ 89/90, 92/93, 94/95, WI 90/91, 94/95, SL 92/93, 94/95, SA 93/94, Sharjah 89/90, WC: NZ 91/92

Test matches: Pak 88/89 (3), WI 88/89 (5), Eng 89 (6), NZ 89/90 (1), SL 89/90 (2), Pak 89/90 (3), NZ 89/90 (1), Eng 90/91 (5), WI 90/91 (5), Ind 91/92 (5), SL 92/93 (3), WI 92/93 (5), NZ 92/93 (3), Eng 93 (6), NZ 93/94 (3), SA 93/94 (3), SA 93/94 (3), Pak 94/95 (2), Eng 94/95 (5)

Highest score against each country:			100s	50s
England	102 *	Old Trafford 93	1	5
India	60	Melbourne 91/92	0	1
New Zealand	113 *	Perth 93/94	1	1
Pakistan	58	Rawalpindi 94/95	0	2
South Africa	61	Cape Town 93/94	0	2
Sri Lanka	71	Moratuwa 92/93	0	2
West Indies	53	Georgetown 90/91	0	2

Coopers & Lybrand world rating (batting): 46= (504)

GRAEME HICK

Full name: Graeme Ashley Hick
Born: 23/05/66   Salisbury (Harare), Zimbabwe
Country: England
Right-hand middle order batsman - Off break bowler
Test debut: 06/06/91 v West Indies - Headingley, Leeds

Test Career Record: *Batting & Fielding*								
Mat	Inns	N/O	Runs	H/S	Avg	100s	50s	Cat
32	56	2	1933	178	35.79	2	11	50
Test Career Record: *Bowling*								
Balls	Runs	Wkts	Avg	Best	5WI	10WM	BPW	
2399	973	19	51.21	4-126	0	0	126.26	

Overseas tours: With Zimbabwe: SL 83/84, Eng 85, WC: Eng 83
With England: NZ 91/92, Ind 92/93, SL 92/93, WI 93/94, Aus 94/95,   WC: Aus & NZ 91/92

Test matches: WI 91 (4), NZ 91/92 (3), Pak 92 (4), Ind 92/93 (3), SL 92/93 (1), Aus 93 (3), WI 93/94 (5), NZ 94 (3), SA 94 (3), Aus 94/95 (3)

Highest score against each country:			100s	50s
Australia	98 *	Sydney 94/95	0	4
India	178	Bombay 92/93	1	1
New Zealand	58	Lord's 94	0	1
Pakistan	51	Edgbaston 92	0	1
South Africa	110	Headingley 94	1	1
Sri Lanka	68	Colombo 92/93	0	1
West Indies	96	Kingston 93/94	0	2

Coopers & Lybrand world rating (batting): 16 (649)

Player Profiles

CARL HOOPER

Full name: Carl Llewellyn Hooper
Born: 15/12/66   Georgetown, Guyana
Country: West Indies
Right-hand middle order batsman - Off break bowler
Test debut: 11/12/87 v India - Wankhede Stadium, Bombay

\multicolumn{9}{l}{**Test Career Record:** *Batting & Fielding*}

Mat	Inns	N/O	Runs	H/S	Avg	100s	50s	Cat
43	73	6	2094	178*	31.25	4	10	47

Test Career Record: *Bowling*

Balls	Runs	Wkts	Avg	Best	5WI	10WM	BPW
5256	2330	45	51.77	5-40	2	0	116.80

Overseas tours: NZ 86/87, Ind 87/88, 93/94, 94/95, Eng 88, 91, Aus 88/89, 91/92, 92/93, Pak 90/91, 91/92, SA 92/93, SL 93/94, Sharjah 88/89, 91/92, 93/94, WC: Ind & Pak 87/88, Aus & NZ 91/92, Young WI: Zim 86/87, 89/90

Test matches: Ind 87/88 (3), Pak 87/88 (3), Eng 88 (5), Aus 88/89 (5), Eng 89/90 (3), Pak 90/91 (3), Aus 90/91 (5), Eng 91 (5), Aus 92/93 (4), Pak 92/93 (3), SL 93/94 (1), Ind 94/95 (3)

Highest score against each country:			100s	50s
Australia	64	Perth 88/89	0	3
England	111	Lord's 91	1	3
India	100*	Calcutta 87/88	1	2
Pakistan	178*	St John's 92/93	2	1
Sri Lanka	62	Moratuwa 93/94	0	1

Coopers & Lybrand world rating (batting): 33 (559)

DAVID HOUGHTON

Full name: David Laud Houghton
Born: 23/06/57 Salisbury (Harare), Zimbabwe
Country: Zimbabwe
Right-hand middle order batsman - Off break bowler
Test debut: 18/10/92 v India - Harare Sports Club

Test Career Record: *Batting & Fielding*								
Mat	Inns	N/O	Runs	H/S	Avg	100s	50s	Cat
13	20	1	912	266	48.00	3	2	9
Test Career Record: *Bowling*								
Balls	Runs	Wkts	Avg	Best	5WI	10WM		BPW
5	0	0	-	-	-	-		-

Overseas tours: Eng 82, 85, 93, SL 83/84, Ind 92/93, 93/94, Pak 93/94, Aus 94/95, Sharjah 92/93, WC: Eng 83, Ind 87/88, Aus & NZ 91/92

Test matches: Ind 92/93 (1), NZ 92/93 (2), Ind 92/93 (1), Pak 93/94 (3), SL 94/95 (3), Pak 94/95 (3)

Highest score against each country:			100s	50s
India	121	Harare 92/93	1	0
New Zealand	36	Bulawayo 92/93	0	0
Pakistan	50	Lahore 93/94	0	1
Sri Lanka	266	Bulawayo 94/95	2	1

Coopers & Lybrand world rating (batting): 25 (598)

ANDREW HUDSON

Full name: Andrew Charles Hudson
Born: 17/03/66   Eshowe, Zululand, South Africa
Country: South Africa
Right-hand middle order batsman - Right-arm medium bowler
Test debut: 18/04/92 v West Indies, Kensington Oval, Bridgetown

Test Career Record: *Batting & Fielding*								
Mat	*Inns*	*N/O*	*Runs*	*H/S*	*Avg*	*100s*	*50s*	*Cat*
18	33	1	1116	163	34.87	2	9	13

Overseas tours: Ind 91/92, 93/94, WI 91/92, SL 93/94, Aus 93/94, Eng 94, Pak 94/95, NZ 94/95, WC: Aus & NZ 91/92

Test matches: WI 91/92 (1), Ind 92/93 (4), SL 93/94 (3), Aus 93/94 (3), Aus 93/94 (3), Eng 94 (2), NZ 94/95 (2)

Highest score against each country:			100s	50s
Australia	102	Cape Town 93/94	1	4
England	12	Headingley 94	0	0
India	55	Durban 92/93	0	3
New Zealand	10	Johannesburg 94/95	0	0
Sri Lanka	90	Moratuwa 93/94	0	2
West Indies	163	Bridgetown 91/92	1	0

Coopers & Lybrand world rating (batting): 49= (487)

MERV HUGHES

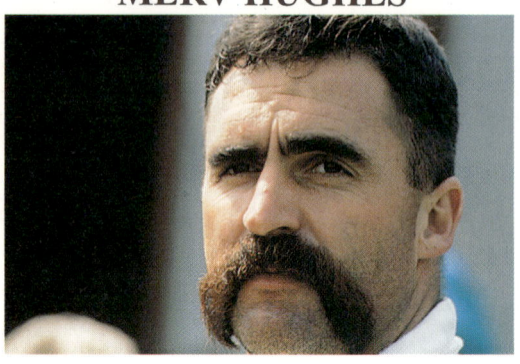

Full name: Mervyn Gregory Hughes
Born: 23/11/61   Euroa, Melbourne, Victoria, Australia
Country: Australia
Right-arm fast medium bowler - Right-hand lower order batsman
Test debut: 13/12/85 v India - Adelaide Oval

Test Career Record: *Batting & Fielding*								
Mat	Inns	N/O	Runs	H/S	Avg	100s	50s	Cat
53	70	8	1032	72*	16.64	0	2	23

Test Career Record: *Bowling*							
Balls	Runs	Wkts	Avg	Best	5WI	10WM	BPW
12285	6017	212	28.38	8-87	7	1	57.94

Overseas tours: Eng 89, 93, Ind 89/90, NZ 89/90, 92/93, WI 90/91, Sharjah: 89/90

Test matches: Ind 85/86 (1), Eng 86/87 (4), NZ 87/88 (1), SL 87/88 (1), WI 88/89 (4), Eng 89 (6), NZ 89/90 (1), SL 89/90 (2), Pak 89/90 (3), Eng 90/91 (4), WI 90/91 (5), Ind 91/92 (5), WI 92/93 (5), NZ 92/93 (3), Eng 93 (6), SA 93/94 (2)

Best bowling against each country:			5WI	10WM
England	5-92	Trent Bridge 93	1	0
India	4-50	Brisbane 91/92	0	0
New Zealand	4-51	Perth 89/90	0	0
Pakistan	5-111	Adelaide 89/90	1	0
South Africa	3-59	Johannesburg 93/94	0	0
Sri Lanka	5-67	Perth 87/88	2	0
West Indies	8-87	Perth 88/89	3	1

Coopers & Lybrand world rating (bowling): 16 (582)

Player Profiles

IJAZ AHMED

Full name: Ijaz Ahmed
Born: 20/09/68   Sialkot, Pakistan
Country: Pakistan
Right-hand middle order batsman - Left-arm medium bowler
Test debut: 03/02/87 v India - Chidambaram Stadium, Chepauk, Madras

Test Career Record: *Batting & Fielding*								
Mat	Inns	N/O	Runs	H/S	Avg	100s	50s	Cat
24	34	0	1056	122	31.05	2	6	20
Test Career Record: *Bowling*								
Balls	Runs	Wkts	Avg	Best	5WI	10WM	BPW	
54	18	1	18.00	1-9	0	0	54.00	

Overseas tours: Aus 86/87, 88/89, 89/90, 91/92, Ind 86/87, 89/90, Eng 87, 92, WI 87/88, NZ 88/89, SA 94/95, Zim 94/95, Ban 88/89, Sharjah 86/87, 88/89, 89/90, 90/91, 91/92, WC: Aus & NZ 91/92, Pak B: Ken 86/87, Pak under 23: SL 84/85

Test matches: Ind 86/87 (1), Eng 87 (4), Eng 87/88 (3), WI 87/88 (2), Aus 88/89 (3), Aus 89/90 (3), NZ 90/91 (3), Aus 94/95 (1), SA 94/95 (1), Zim 94/95 (3)

Highest score against each country:			100s	50s
Australia	122	Faisalabad 88/89	2	0
England	69	The Oval 87	0	2
India	3	Madras 86/87	0	0
New Zealand	86	Lahore 90/91	0	1
South Africa	19	Johannesburg 94/95	0	0
West Indies	43	Port of Spain 87/88	0	0
Zimbabwe	76	Bulawayo 94/95	0	3

Coopers & Lybrand world rating (batting): 41 (514)

INZAMAM-UL-HAQ

Full name: Inzamam-ul-Haq
Born: 03/03/70   Multan, Pakistan
Country: Pakistan
Right-hand middle order batsman - Left-arm slow bowler
Test debut: 04/06/92 v England - Edgbaston, Birmingham

Test Career Record: *Batting & Fielding*								
Mat	*Inns*	*N/O*	*Runs*	*H/S*	*Avg*	*100s*	*50s*	*Cat*
23	39	7	1541	135*	48.15	4	9	22

Overseas tours: Aus 91/92, 92/93, Eng 92, NZ 92/93, 93/94, WI 92/93, SA 92/93, 94/95, SL 94/95, Zim 94/95, Sharjah 92/93, 93/94, WC: Aus & NZ 91/92, Pak A: SL 90/91

Test matches: Eng 92 (4), NZ 92/93 (1), WI 92/93 (3), Zim 93/94 (3), NZ 93/94 (3), SL 94/95 (2), Aus 94/95 (3), SA 94/95 (1), Zim 94/95 (3)

Highest score against each country:			100s	50s
Australia	66	Lahore 94/95	0	2
England	26	Old Trafford 92	0	0
New Zealand	135*	Wellington 93/94	1	1
South Africa	95	Johannesburg 94/95	0	1
Sri Lanka	100*	Kandy 94/95	1	1
West Indies	123	St John's 92/93	1	0
Zimbabwe	101	Harare 94/95	1	4

Coopers & Lybrand world rating (batting): 2 (868)

Player Profiles

ANDREW JONES

Full name: Andrew Howard Jones
Born: 09/05/59   Wellington, New Zealand
Country: New Zealand
Right-hand middle order batsman - Off break bowler
Test debut: 16/04/87 v Sri Lanka - Colombo Cricket Club Ground

Test Career Record: *Batting & Fielding*								
Mat	Inns	N/O	Runs	H/S	Avg	100s	50s	Cat
39	74	8	2922	186	44.27	7	11	24
Test Career Record: *Bowling*								
Balls	Runs	Wkts	Avg	Best	5WI	10WM		BPW
322	189	1	189.00	1-40	0	0		322.00

Overseas tours: SL 86/87, 92/93, Aus 87/88, 89/90, 90/91, 93/94, Ind 88/89, Eng 90, Zim 92/93, Sharjah 87/88, 89/90, WC: Ind 87/88

Test matches: SL 86/87 (1), Aus 87/88 (3), Eng 87/88 (1), Ind 88/89 (3), Pak 88/89 (2), Ind 89/90 (3), Aus 89/90 (1), Eng 90 (3), SL 90/91 (3), Eng 91/92 (3), Zim 92/93 (2), SL 92/93 (2), Pak 92/93 (1), Aus 92/93 (3), Aus 93/94 (3), Pak 93/94 (3), WI 94/95 (2)

Highest score against each country:			100s	50s
Australia	150	Adelaide 87/88	2	2
England	143	Wellington 91/92	1	1
India	170	Auckland 89/90	1	2
Pakistan	86	Wellington 88/89	0	4
Sri Lanka	186	Wellington 90/91	3	1
West Indies	12	Christchurch 94/95	0	0
Zimbabwe	67*	Bulawayo 92/93	0	1

Coopers & Lybrand world rating (batting): 31= (563)

The Test Cricketer's Almanac

VINOD KAMBLI

Full name: Vinod Ganpat Kambli
Born: 18/01/72   Bombay, India
Country: India
Left-hand middle order batsman - Off break bowler
Test debut: 29/01/93 v England - Eden Gardens, Calcutta

\multicolumn{9}{l}{**Test Career Record:** *Batting & Fielding*}
Mat	Inns	N/O	Runs	H/S	Avg	100s	50s	Cat
14	19	1	1029	227	57.16	4	3	6

Overseas tours: SA 92/93, SL 93/94, 94/95, NZ 93/94, 94/95, Sharjah 91/92, 93/94

Test matches: Eng 92/93 (3), Zim 92/93 (1), SL 93/94 (3), SL 93/94 (3), NZ 93/94 (1), WI 94/95 (3)

Highest score against each country:			100s	50s
England	224	Bombay 92/93	1	1
New Zealand	19	Hamilton 93/94	0	0
Sri Lanka	125	Colombo 93/94	2	2
West Indies	40	Bombay 94/95	0	0
Zimbabwe	227	Delhi 92/93	1	0

Coopers & Lybrand world rating (batting): 26 (590*)

Player Profiles

KAPIL DEV

Full name: Kapil Dev Ramlal Nikhanj
Born: 06/01/59   Chandigarh, India
Country: India
Right-arm fast medium bowler - Right-hand middle order batsman
Test debut: 16/10/78 v Pakistan - Iqbal Stadium, Faisalabad

Test Career Record: *Batting & Fielding*								
Mat	Inns	N/O	Runs	H/S	Avg	100s	50s	Cat
131	184	15	5248	163	31.05	8	27	64

Test Career Record: *Bowling*							
Balls	Runs	Wkts	Avg	Best	5WI	10WM	BPW
27740	12867	434	29.64	9-83	23	2	63.91

Overseas tours: Pak 78/79, 82/83, 84/85, 89/90, Eng 79, 82, 86, 90, Aus 80/81, 84/85, 85/86, 91/92, NZ 80/81, 89/90, 93/94, WI 82/83, 88/89, SL 85/86, 93/94, 94/95, Zim 92/93, SA 92/93, Ban 88/89, Sharjah 84/85, 85/86, 86/87, 87/88, 88/89, 89/90, 91/92, WC: Eng 79, 83, Aus & NZ 91/92, RW: Eng 87, 91

Test matches: Pak 78/79 (3), WI 78/79 (6), Eng 79 (4), Aus 79/80 (6), Pak 79/80 (6), Eng 79/80 (1), Aus 80/81 (3), NZ 80/81 (3), Eng 81/82 (6), Eng 82 (3), SL 82/83 (1), Pak 82/83 (6), WI 82/83 (5), Pak 83/84 (3), WI 83/84 (6), Pak 84/85 (2), Eng 84/85 (4), SL 85/86 (3), Aus 85/86 (3), Eng 86 (3), Aus 86/87 (3), SL 86/87 (3), Pak 86/87 (5), WI 87/88 (4), NZ 88/89 (3), WI 88/89 (4), Pak 89/90 (4), NZ 89/90 (3), Eng 90 (3), SL 90/91 (1), Aus 91/92 (5), Zim 92/93 (1), S/A 92/93 (4), Eng 92/93 (3), Zim 92/93 (1), SL 93/94 (3), SL 93/94 (3), NZ 93/94 (1)

Best bowling against each country:			5WI	10WM
Australia	8-106	Adelaide 85/86	7	0
England	6-91	Calcutta 81/82	4	0
New Zealand	4-34	Wellington 80/81	0	0
Pakistan	8-85	Lahore 82/83	7	1
South Africa	3-43	Durban 92/93	0	0
Sri Lanka	5-110	Madras 82/83	1	0
West Indies	9-83	Ahmedabad 83/84	4	1
Zimbabwe	2-22	Harare 92/93	0	0

Player Profiles

GARY KIRSTEN

Full name: Gary Kirsten
Born: 23/11/67　　Cape Town, South Africa
Country: South Africa
Left-hand opening batsman - Off break bowler
Test debut: 26/12/93 v Australia - Melbourne Cricket Ground

Test Career Record: *Batting & Fielding*								
Mat	*Inns*	*N/O*	*Runs*	*H/S*	*Avg*	*100s*	*50s*	*Cat*
13	24	1	856	72	37.21	0	6	14
Test Career Record: *Bowling*								
Balls	*Runs*	*Wkts*	*Avg*	*Best*	*5WI*	*10WM*		*BPW*
289	133	2	66.50	1-0	0	0		144.50

Overseas tours: Aus 93/94, Eng 94, Pak 94/95, NZ 94/95

Test matches: Aus 93/94 (3), Aus 93/94 (3), Eng 94 (3), NZ 94/95 (3), Pak 94/95 (1)

Highest score against each country:			100s	50s
Australia	67	Sydney 93/94	0	1
England	72	Lord's 94	0	2
New Zealand	66 *	Durban 94/95	0	2
Pakistan	62	Johannesburg 94/95	0	1

Coopers & Lybrand world rating (batting): 11 (670)

PETER KIRSTEN

Full name: Peter Noel Kirsten
Born: 14/05/55   Pietermaritzburg, South Africa
Country: South Africa
Right-hand middle order batsman - Off break bowler
Test debut: 18/04/92 v West Indies - Kensington Oval, Bridgetown

\multicolumn{9}{l}{**Test Career Record:** *Batting & Fielding*}

Test Career Record: *Batting & Fielding*
Mat	Inns	N/O	Runs	H/S	Avg	100s	50s	Cat
12	22	2	626	104	31.30	1	4	9

Test Career Record: *Bowling*
Balls	Runs	Wkts	Avg	Best	5WI	10WM	BPW
54	30	0	-	-	-	-	-

Overseas tours: Ind 91/92, WI 91/92, Aus 93/94, Eng 94, WC: Aus & NZ 91/92

Test matches: WI 91/92 (1), Ind 92/93 (4), Aus 93/94 (1), Aus 93/94 (3), Eng 94 (3)

Highest score against each country:			100s	50s
Australia	79	Adelaide 93/94	0	3
England	104	Headingley 94	1	0
India	26	Johannesburg 92/93	0	0
West Indies	52	Bridgetown 91/92	0	1

Coopers & Lybrand world rating (batting): 44 (507)

Player Profiles

ANIL KUMBLE

Full name: Anil Radhakrishna Kumble
Born: 17/10/70   Bangalore, India
Country: India
Leg break & googly bowler - Right-hand lower order batsman
Test debut: 09/08/90 v England - Old Trafford, Manchester

Test Career Record: *Batting & Fielding*								
Mat	Inns	N/O	Runs	H/S	Avg	100s	50s	Cat
20	21	4	249	52*	14.64	0	1	9
Test Career Record: *Bowling*								
Balls	Runs	Wkts	Avg	Best	5WI	10WM		BPW
6567	2510	99	25.35	7-59	5	1		66.33

Overseas tours: Eng 90, Zim 92/93, SA 92/93, SL 93/94, 94/95, NZ 93/94, 94/95, Sharjah 89/90, 91/92, 93/94

Test matches: Eng 90 (1), Zim 92/93 (1), SA 92/93 (4), Eng 92/93 (3), Zim 92/93 (1), SL 93/94 (3), SL 93/94 (3), NZ 93/94 (1), WI 94/95 (3)

Best bowling against each country:			5WI	10WM
England	6-64	Madras 92/93	1	0
New Zealand	1-34	Hamilton 93/94	0	0
South Africa	6-53	Johannesburg 92/93	1	0
Sri Lanka	7-59	Lucknow 93/94	2	1
West Indies	4-90	Chandigarh 94/95	0	0
Zimbabwe	5-70	Delhi 92/93	1	0

Coopers & Lybrand world rating (bowling): 6 (797)

BRIAN LARA

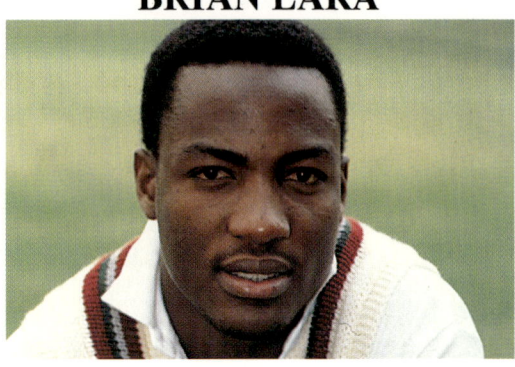

Full name: Brian Charles Lara
Born: 02/05/69   Santa Cruz, Trinidad
Country: West Indies
Left-hand middle order batsman - Leg break & googly bowler
Test debut: 06/12/90 v Pakistan - Gaddafi Stadium, Lahore

Test Career Record: *Batting & Fielding*

Mat	Inns	N/O	Runs	H/S	Avg	100s	50s	Cat
21	34	0	1975	375	58.08	4	10	33

Test Career Record: *Bowling*

Balls	Runs	Wkts	Avg	Best	5WI	10WM	BPW
36	12	0	-	-	-	-	-

Overseas tours: Pak 90/91, 91/92, Eng 91, Aus 91/92, 92/93, SA 92/93, Ind 93/94, 94/95, SL 93/94, NZ 94/95, Sharjah 91/92, 93/94, WC: Aus & NZ 91/92, Young WI: Zim 89/90

Test matches: Pak 90/91 (1), SA 91/92 (1), Aus 92/93 (5), Pak 92/93 (3), SL 93/94 (1), Eng 93/94 (5), Ind 94/95 (3), NZ 94/95 (2)

Highest score against each country:			100s	50s
Australia	277	Sydney 92/93	1	3
England	375	St John's 93/94	2	2
India	91	Chandigarh 94/95	0	2
New Zealand	147	Wellington 94/95	1	0
Pakistan	96	Port of Spain 92/93	0	2
South Africa	64	Bridgetown 91/92	0	1
Sri Lanka	18	Moratuwa 93/94	0	0

Coopers & Lybrand world rating (batting): 3 (794)

Player Profiles

CHRIS LEWIS

Full name: Clairmonte Christopher Lewis
Born: 14/02/68   Georgetown, Guyana
Country: England
Right-arm fast medium bowler - Right-hand middle order batsman
Test debut: 05/07/90 v New Zealand - Edgbaston, Birmingham

Test Career Record: *Batting & Fielding*								
Mat	Inns	N/O	Runs	H/S	Avg	100s	50s	Cat
27	44	2	1009	117	24.02	1	4	23

Test Career Record: *Bowling*							
Balls	Runs	Wkts	Avg	Best	5WI	10WM	BPW
5636	2870	77	37.27	6-111	2	0	73.19

Overseas tours: WI 89/90, 93/94, Aus 90/91, 94/95, NZ 91/92, Ind 92/93, SL 92/93, WC: Aus & NZ 91/92, Eng A: Zim 89/90

Test matches: NZ 90 (1), Ind 90 (2), Aus 90/91 (1), WI 91 (2), SL 91 (1), NZ 91/92 (2), Pak 92 (5), Ind 92/93 (3), SL 92/93 (1), Aus 93 (2), WI 93/94 (5), Aus 94/95 (2)

Best bowling against each country:			5WI	10WM
Australia	4-24	Adelaide 94/95	0	0
India	2-26	Lord's 90	0	0
New Zealand	5-31	Auckland 91/92	1	0
Pakistan	3-43	Lord's 92	0	0
Sri Lanka	4-66	Colombo 92/93	0	0
West Indies	6-111	Edgbaston 91	1	0

Coopers & Lybrand world rating (bowling): 27 (445)

ROSHAN MAHANAMA

Full name: Roshan Siriwardene Mahanama
Born: 31/05/66   Colombo, Sri Lanka
Country: Sri Lanka
Right-hand opening batsman
Test debut: 14/03/86 v Pakistan   P. Saravanamuttu Stadium, Colombo

Test Career Record: Batting & Fielding								
Mat	Inns	N/O	Runs	H/S	Avg	100s	50s	Cat
32	53	0	1687	153	31.83	3	9	19
Test Career Record: *Bowling*								
Balls	Runs	Wkts	Avg	Best	5WI	10WM		BPW
36	30	0	-	-	-	-		-

Overseas tours: Ind 86/87, 89/90, 90/91, 93/94, Aus 87/88, 89/90, Eng 88, 90, 91, NZ 90/91, Pak 91/92, Zim 94/95, SA 94/95, Ban 88/89, Sharjah 85/86, 86/87, 87/88, 88/89, 90/91, 92/93, 93/94, WC: Ind & Pak 87/88, Aus & NZ 92/93

Test matches: Pak 85/86 (2), NZ 86/87 (1), Aus 87/88 (1), Aus 89/90 (2), Ind 90/91 (1), NZ 90/91 (1), Eng 91 (1), Pak 91/92 (2), Aus 92/93 (3), NZ 92/93 (2), Eng 92/93 (1), Ind 93/94 (3), SA 93/94 (3), WI 93/94 (1), Ind 93/94 (3), Pak 94/95 (2), Zim 94/95 (3)

Highest score against each country:			100s	50s
Australia	85	Hobart 89/90	0	4
England	64	Colombo 92/93	0	1
India	151	Colombo 93/94	1	2
New Zealand	153	Moratuwa 92/93	2	0
Pakistan	58	Faisalabad 91/92	0	1
South Africa	53	Moratuwa 93/94	0	1
West Indies	11	Moratuwa 93/94	0	0
Zimbabwe	24	Harare 94/95	0	0

Coopers & Lybrand world rating (batting): 55 (454)

Player Profiles

DEVON MALCOLM

Full name: Devon Eugene Malcolm
Born: 22/02/63   Kingston, Jamaica
Country: England
Right-arm fast bowler - Right-hand lower order batsman
Test debut: 10/08/89 v Australia - Trent Bridge, Nottingham

Test Career Record: *Batting & Fielding*								
Mat	Inns	N/O	Runs	H/S	Avg	100s	50s	Cat
32	47	16	208	29	6.70	0	0	5
Test Career Record: *Bowling*								
Balls	Runs	Wkts	Avg	Best	5WI	10WM		BPW
7277	4026	111	36.27	9-57	5	2		65.55

Overseas tours: WI 89/90, 93/94, Aus 90/91, 94/95, Ind 92/93, SL 92/93, Eng A: WI 91/92

Test matches: Aus 89 (1), WI 89/90 (4), NZ 90 (3), Ind 90 (3), Aus 90/91 (5), WI 91 (2), Pak 92 (3), Ind 92/93 (2), SL 92/93 (1), Aus 93 (1), WI 93/94 (1), NZ 94 (1), SA 94 (1), Aus 94/95 (4)

Best bowling against each country:			5WI	10WM
Australia	4-39	Adelaide 94/95	0	0
India	3-67	Calcutta 92/93	0	0
New Zealand	5-46	Edgbaston 90	2	0
Pakistan	5-94	The Oval 92	1	0
South Africa	9-57	The Oval 94	1	1
Sri Lanka	0-11	Colombo 92/93	0	0
West Indies	6-77	Port of Spain 89/90	1	1

Coopers & Lybrand world rating (bowling): 23 (491)

SANJAY MANJREKAR

Full name: Sanjay Vijay Manjrekar
Born: 12/07/65   Mangalore, India
Country: India
Right-hand middle order batsman - Off break bowler
Test debut: 25/11/87 v West Indies - Feroz Shah Kotla, Delhi

Test Career Record: *Batting & Fielding*									
Mat	Inns	N/O	Runs	H/S	Avg	100s	50s	Cat	St
33	53	5	1855	218	38.64	4	8	22	1
Test Career Record: *Bowling*									
Balls	Runs	Wkts	Avg	Best	5WI	10WM	BPW		
17	15	0	-	-	-	-	-		

Overseas tours: WI 88/89, Pak 89/90, NZ 89/90, 93/94, 94/95, Eng 90, Aus 91/92, Zim 92/93, SA 92/93, Sharjah 89/90, 91/92, WC: Aus & NZ 91/92, RW: Eng 91

Test matches: WI 87/88 (1), WI 88/89 (4), Pak 89/90 (4), NZ 89/90 (3), Eng 90 (3), SL 90/91 (1), Aus 91/92 (5), Zim 92/93 (1), SA 92/93 (4), SL 93/94 (3), NZ 93/94 (1), WI 94/95 (3)

Highest score against each country:			100s	50s
England	93	Old Trafford 90	0	2
New Zealand	42	Napier 89/90	0	0
Pakistan	218	Lahore 89/90	2	3
South Africa	46	Cape Town 92/93	0	0
Sri Lanka	61	Lucknow 93/94	0	1
West Indies	108	Bridgetown 88/89	1	2
Zimbabwe	104	Harare 92/93	1	0

Coopers & Lybrand world rating (batting): 49= (487)

CRAIG MATTHEWS

Full name: Craig Russell Matthews
Born: 15/02/65 Cape Town, South Africa
Country: South Africa
Right-arm fast medium bowler - Right-hand middle order batsman
Test debut: 26/11/92 v India - Wanderers Stadium, Johannesburg

Test Career Record: *Batting & Fielding*

Mat	Inns	N/O	Runs	H/S	Avg	100s	50s	Cat
13	19	5	288	62*	20.57	0	1	0

Test Career Record: *Bowling*

Balls	Runs	Wkts	Avg	Best	5WI	10WM	BPW
3027	1142	41	27.85	5-42	2	0	73.82

Overseas tours: Aus 93/94, Eng 94, Pak 94/95, NZ 94/95

Test matches: Ind 92/93 (3), Aus 93/94 (2), Aus 93/94 (3), Eng 94 (3), NZ 94/95 (2)

Best bowling against each country:			5WI	10WM
Australia	5-80	Cape Town 93/94	1	0
England	3-25	Lord's 94	0	0
India	3-32	Cape Town 92/93	0	0
New Zealand	5-42	Johannesburg 94/95	1	0

Coopers & Lybrand world rating (bowling): 19 (252*)

TIM MAY

Full name: Timothy Brian Alexander May
Born: 26/01/62   North Adelaide, South Australia
Country: Australia
Off break bowler - Right-hand lower order batsman
Test debut: 11/12/87 v New Zealand - Adelaide Oval

Test Career Record: *Batting & Fielding*								
Mat	Inns	N/O	Runs	H/S	Avg	100s	50s	Cat
24	28	12	225	42*	14.06	0	0	6
Test Career Record: *Bowling*								
Balls	Runs	Wkts	Avg	Best	5WI	10WM		BPW
6577	2606	75	34.74	5-9	3	0		87.69

Overseas tours: Pak 88/89, 94/95, Eng 89, 93, Ind 89/90, NZ 92/93, 94/95, SA 93/94, SL 94/95, WI 94/95, Sharjah 93/94, WC: Ind & Pak 87/88

Test matches: NZ 87/88 (1), Pak 88/89 (3), WI 88/89 (3), WI 92/93 (1), Eng 93 (5), NZ 93/94 (2), SA 93/94 (3), SA 93/94 (1), Pak 94/95 (2), Eng 94/95 (3)

Best bowling against each country:			5WI	10WM
England	5-89	Edgbaston 93	1	0
New Zealand	5-65	Hobart 93/94	1	0
Pakistan	4-97	Karachi 88/89	0	0
South Africa	2-26	Adelaide 93/94	0	0
West Indies	5-9	Adelaide 92/93	1	0

Coopers & Lybrand world rating (bowling): 30 (405)

CRAIG MCDERMOTT

Full name: Craig John McDermott
Born: 14/04/65   Ipswich, Queensland, Australia
Country: Australia
Right-arm fast bowler - Right-hand lower order batsman
Test debut: 22/12/84 v West Indies - Melbourne C. G.

Test Career Record: *Batting & Fielding*								
Mat	Inns	N/O	Runs	H/S	Avg	100s	50s	Cat
65	84	12	897	42*	12.45	0	0	15
Test Career Record: *Bowling*								
Balls	Runs	Wkts	Avg	Best	5WI	10WM		BPW
15385	7697	270	28.50	8-97	13	2		56.98

Overseas tours: Eng 85, 93, NZ 85/86, 92/93, Ind 86/87, Pak 89/90, 94/95, WI 90/91, 94/95, SL 92/93, 94/95, SA 93/94, Sharjah 84/85, 85/86, WC: Ind & Pak 87/88, NZ 91/92

Test matches: WI 84/85 (2), Eng 85 (6), NZ 85/86 (2), Ind 85/86 (2), NZ 85/86 (2), Ind 86/87 (2), Eng 86/87 (1), NZ 87/88 (3), Eng 87/88 (1), SL 87/88 (1), WI 88/89 (2), Eng 90/91 (2), WI 90/91 (5), Ind 91/92 (5), SL 92/93 (3), WI 92/93 (5), NZ 92/93 (3), Eng 93 (2), NZ 93/94 (3), SA 93/94 (3), SA 93/94 (3), Pak 94/95 (2), Eng 94/95 (5)

Best bowling against each country:			5WI	10WM
England	8-97	Perth 90/91	8	1
India	5-54	Brisbane 91/92	3	1
New Zealand	5-97	Melbourne 87/88	1	0
Pakistan	4-74	Rawalpindi 94/95	0	0
South Africa	4-33	Adelaide 93/94	0	0
Sri Lanka	4-53	Colombo 92/93	0	0
West Indies	5-80	Kingston 90/91	1	0

Coopers & Lybrand world rating (bowling): 9 (719)

GLENN MCGRATH

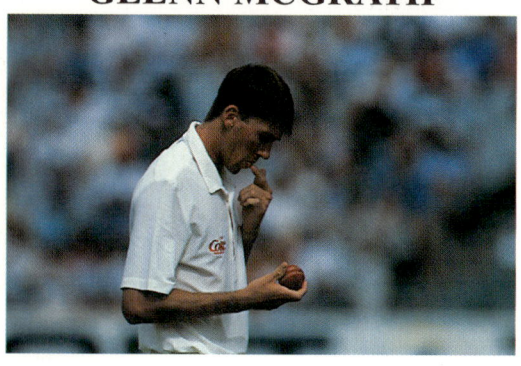

Full name: Glenn Donald McGrath
Born: 09/02/70   Dubbo, New South Wales, Australia
Country: Australia
Right-arm fast bowler - Right-hand lower order batsman
Test debut: 12/11/93 v New Zealand - WACA Ground, Perth

Test Career Record: *Batting & Fielding*								
Mat	Inns	N/O	Runs	H/S	Avg	100s	50s	Cat
9	10	2	15	9	1.87	0	0	0
Test Career Record: *Bowling*								
Balls	Runs	Wkts	Avg	Best	5WI	10WM		BPW
2156	958	25	38.32	4-92	0	0		86.24

Overseas tours: SA 93/94, SL 94/95, Pak 94/95, NZ 94/95, WI 94/95, Sharjah 93/94

Test matches: NZ 93/94 (2), SA 93/94 (3), Pak 94/95 (2), Eng 94/95 (2)

Best bowling against each country:			5WI	10WM
England	3-40	Perth 94/95	0	0
New Zealand	3-66	Brisbane 93/94	0	0
Pakistan	4-92	Lahore 94/95	0	0
South Africa	3-65	Cape Town 93/94	0	0

Coopers & Lybrand world rating (bowling): 40 (324*)

Player Profiles

BRIAN MCMILLAN

Full name: Brian Mervin McMillan
Born: 22/12/63 Welkom, South Africa
Country: South Africa
Right-arm fast medium bowler - Right-hand middle order batsman
Test debut: 13/11/92 v India - Kingsmead, Durban

Test Career Record: *Batting & Fielding*								
Mat	Inns	N/O	Runs	H/S	Avg	100s	50s	Cat
17	27	3	879	113	36.62	1	6	21

Test Career Record: *Bowling*							
Balls	Runs	Wkts	Avg	Best	5WI	10WM	BPW
3464	1476	51	28.94	4-65	0	0	67.92

Overseas tours: Ind 91/92, 93/94, SL 93/94, Aus 93/94, Eng 94, Pak 94/95, NZ 94/95, WC: Aus & NZ 91/92

Test matches: Ind 92/93 (4), SL 93/94 (2), Aus 93/94 (1), Aus 93/94 (3), Eng 94 (3), NZ 94/95 (3), Pak 94/95 (1)

Best bowling against each country:			5WI	10WM
Australia	3-61	Johannesburg 93/94	0	0
England	3-16	Lord's 94	0	0
India	4-74	Johannesburg 92/93	0	0
New Zealand	4-65	Cape Town 94/95	0	0
Pakistan	2-33	Johannesburg 94/95	0	0
Sri Lanka	1-11	Colombo 93/94	0	0

Coopers & Lybrand world rating (bowling): 13 (669)

MOIN KHAN

Full name: Moin Khan
Born: 23/09/71   Rawalpindi, Pakistan
Country: Pakistan
Right-hand middle order batsman - Wicket-Keeper
Test debut: 23/11/90 v West Indies - Iqbal Stadium, Faisalabad

Test Career Record: Batting & Fielding									
Mat	Inns	N/O	Runs	H/S	Avg	100s	50s	Cat	St
13	19	3	309	115*	19.31	1	0	34	2

Overseas tours: Aus 91/92, Eng 92, SA 94/95, Sharjah 91/92, WC: Aus & NZ 91/92, Pak A: SL 90/91, Pak B: Zim 90/91

Test matches: WI 90/91 (2), SL 91/92 (3), Eng 92 (4), WI 92/93 (2), Aus 94/95 (1), SA 94/95 (1)

Highest score against each country:			100s	50s
Australia	115*	Lahore 94/95	1	0
England	15	Old Trafford 92	0	0
South Africa	9	Johannesburg 94/95	0	0
Sri Lanka	22*	Faisalabad 91/92	0	0
West Indies	32	Faisalabad 90/91	0	0

Coopers & Lybrand world rating (batting): 83 (280*)

Player Profiles

NAYAN MONGIA

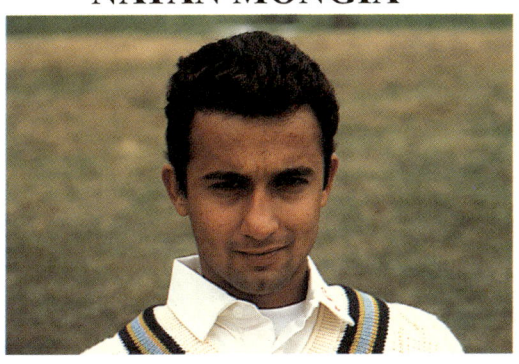

Full name: Nayan Ramlal Mongia
Born: 19/12/69   Baroda, India
Country: India
Right-hand middle order batsman - Wicket-Keeper
Test debut: 18/01/94 v Sri Lanka - Babu Stadium, Lucknow

Test Career Record: *Batting & Fielding*									
Mat	Inns	N/O	Runs	H/S	Avg	100s	50s	Cat	St
7	11	1	342	80	34.20	0	1	16	2

Overseas tours: Eng 90, NZ 93/94, 94/95, SL 94/95, Sharjah 93/94

Test matches: SL 93/94 (3), NZ 93/94 (1), WI 94/95 (3)

Highest score against each country:			100s	50s
New Zealand	45	Hamilton 93/94	0	0
Sri Lanka	44	Lucknow 93/94	0	0
West Indies	80	Bombay 94/95	0	1

Coopers & Lybrand world rating (batting): 72 (324*)

DANNY MORRISON

Full name: Daniel Kyle Morrison
Born: 03/02/66   Auckland, New Zealand
Country: New Zealand
Right-arm fast medium bowler - Right-hand lower order batsman
Test debut: 04/12/87 v Australia - Woolloongabba, Brisbane

Test Career Record: *Batting & Fielding*								
Mat	Inns	N/O	Runs	H/S	Avg	100s	50s	Cat
39	57	19	311	42	8.18	0	0	13
Test Career Record: *Bowling*							
Balls	Runs	Wkts	Avg	Best	5WI	10WM	BPW
8332	4563	133	34.30	7-89	9	0	62.64

Overseas tours: SL 86/87, 92/93, Aus 87/88, 89/90, 90/91, 93/94, Ind 88/89, Eng 90, Pak 90/91, Zim 92/93, SA 94/95, Sharjah 87/88, 89/90, 93/94, WC: Ind 87/88, Young NZ: Zim 88/89, RW: Eng 91, 93

Test matches: Aus 87/88 (3), Eng 87/88 (3), Ind 88/89 (1), Pak 88/89 (1), Aus 89/90 (1), Ind 89/90 (3), Aus 89/90 (1), Eng 90 (3), Pak 90/91 (3), SL 90/91 (3), Eng 91/92 (3), Pak 92/93 (1), Aus 92/93 (3), Aus 93/94 (3), Pak 93/94 (2), Ind 93/94 (1), SA 94/95 (2), WI 94/95 (2)

Best bowling against each country:			5WI	10WM
Australia	7-89	Wellington 92/93	2	0
England	5-69	Christchurch 87/88	1	0
India	5-75	Christchurch 89/90	3	0
Pakistan	5-41	Hamilton 92/93	1	0
South Africa	4-70	Durban 94/95	0	0
Sri Lanka	5-153	Wellington 90/91	1	0
West Indies	6-69	Christchurch 94/95	1	0

Coopers & Lybrand world rating (bowling): 18 (532)

Player Profiles

MUTTIAH MURALITHARAN

Full name: Muttiah Muralitharan
Born: 17/04/72   Kandy, Sri Lanka
Country: Sri Lanka
Right-hand lower order batsman - Off break bowler
Test debut: 28/08/92 v Australia - Khettarama Stadium, Colombo

Test Career Record: Batting & Fielding

Mat	Inns	N/O	Runs	H/S	Avg	100s	50s	Cat
16	18	11	128	20*	18.28	0	0	6

Test Career Record: Bowling

Balls	Runs	Wkts	Avg	Best	5WI	10WM	BPW
4203	1846	56	32.96	5-101	3	0	75.05

Overseas tours: Eng 91, Ind 93/94, Zim 94/95, SA 94/95, Sharjah 93/94, SL under 24: SA 92/93

Test matches: Aus 92/93 (2), NZ 92/93 (1), Eng 92/93 (1), Ind 93/94 (2), SA 93/94 (3), WI 93/94 (1), Ind 93/94 (3), Pak 94/95 (1), Zim 94/95 (2)

Best bowling against each country:			5WI	10WM
Australia	2-109	Colombo 92/93	0	0
England	4-118	Colombo 92/93	0	0
India	5-162	Lucknow 93/94	1	0
New Zealand	4-134	Colombo 92/93	0	0
Pakistan	1-123	Colombo 94/95	0	0
South Africa	5-101	Colombo 93/94	2	0
West Indies	4-47	Moratuwa 93/94	0	0
Zimbabwe	2-60	Harare 94/95	0	0

Coopers & Lybrand world rating (bowling): 22 (509)

JUNIOR MURRAY

Full name: Junior Randalph Murray
Born: 20/01/68   St George's, Grenada
Country: West Indies
Right hand middle order batsman - Wicket-Keeper
Test debut: 02/01/93 v Australia - Sydney Cricket Ground

Test Career Record: *Batting & Fielding*									
Mat	Inns	N/O	Runs	H/S	Avg	100s	50s	Cat	St
17	21	3	545	101*	30.27	1	2	60	2

Overseas tours: Aus 92/93, SA 92/93, Ind 93/94, 94/95, SL 93/94, NZ 94/95, Sharjah 93/94

Test matches: Aus 92/93 (3), Pak 92/93 (3), SL 93/94 (1), Eng 93/94 (5), Ind 94/95 (3), NZ 94/95 (2)

Highest score against each country:			100s	50s
Australia	49*	Adelaide 92/93	0	0
England	34	Kingston 93/94	0	0
India	85	Bombay 94/95	0	2
New Zealand	101*	Wellington 94/95	1	0
Pakistan	35	Bridgetown 92/93	0	0
Sri Lanka	7	Moratuwa 93/94	0	0

Coopers & Lybrand world rating (batting): 45 (505)

Player Profiles

MUSHTAQ AHMED

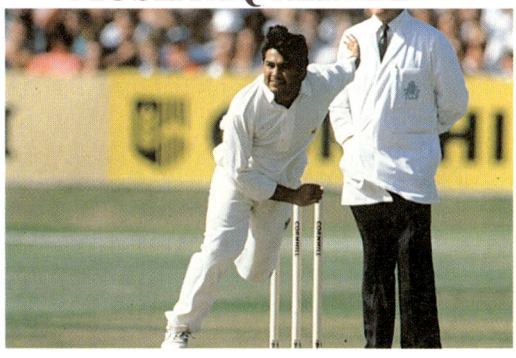

Full name: Mushtaq Ahmed
Born: 28/06/70   Sahiwal, Pakistan
Country: Pakistan
Leg break & googly bowler - Right-hand lower order batsman
Test debut: 19/01/90 v Australia - Adelaide Oval

\multicolumn{9}{l}{Test Career Record: *Batting & Fielding*}

Mat	Inns	N/O	Runs	H/S	Avg	100s	50s	Cat
18	26	6	163	27	8.15	0	0	5

Test Career Record: *Bowling*

Balls	Runs	Wkts	Avg	Best	5WI	10WM	BPW
3338	1605	44	36.47	4-121	0	0	75.86

Overseas tours: Ind 89/90, Aus 89/90, 91/92, 92/93, Eng 92, NZ 92/93, 93/94, WI 92/93, SA 92/93, Zim 92/93, SL 94/95, Sharjah 88/89, 89/90, 90/91, 91/92, 92/93, 93/94, WC: Aus & NZ 91/92

Test matches: Aus 89/90 (1), WI 90/91 (2), Eng 92 (5), NZ 92/93 (1), WI 92/93 (1), Zim 93/94 (2), NZ 93/94 (1), SL 94/95 (2), Aus 94/95 (3)

Best bowling against each country:			5WI	10WM
Australia	4-121	Lahore 94/95	0	0
England	3-32	Lord's 92	0	0
New Zealand	3-79	Auckland 93/94	0	0
Sri Lanka	3-34	Kandy 94/95	0	0
West Indies	2-56	Karachi 90/91	0	0
Zimbabwe	2-24	Karachi 93/94	0	0

Coopers & Lybrand world rating (bowling): 28 (413*)

DION NASH

Full name: Dion Joseph Nash
Born: 20/11/71   Auckland, New Zealand
Country: New Zealand
Right-arm medium bowler - Right-hand middle order batsman
Test debut: 07/11/92 v Zimbabwe - Harare Sports Club

Test Career Record: Batting & Fielding								
Mat	Inns	N/O	Runs	H/S	Avg	100s	50s	Cat
8	12	5	169	56	24.14	0	1	6
Test Career Record: *Bowling*							
Balls	Runs	Wkts	Avg	Best	5WI	10WM	BPW
1518	760	24	31.66	6-76	2	1	63.25

Overseas tours: Zim 92/93, SL 92/93, Eng 94, Ind 94/95, SA 94/95, Sharjah 93/94

Test matches: Zim 92/93 (1), SL 92/93 (1), Ind 93/94 (1), Eng 94 (3), SA 94/95 (1), WI 94/95 (1)

Best bowling against each country:			5WI	10WM
England	6-76	Lord's 94	2	1
India	1-57	Hamilton 93/94	0	0
South Africa	3-81	Johannesburg 94/95	0	0
Sri Lanka	1-62	Moratuwa 92/93	0	0
West Indies	0-11	Christchurch 94/95	0	0
Zimbabwe	1-19	Harare 92/93	0	0

Coopers & Lybrand world rating (bowling): 35 (359*)

ADAM PARORE

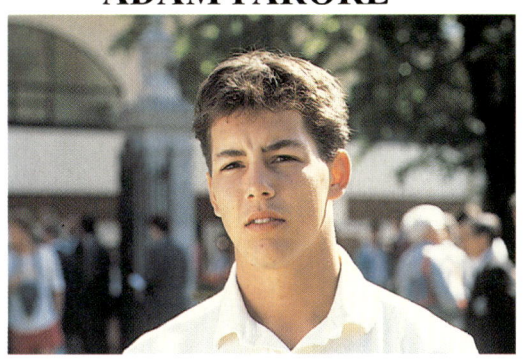

Full name: Adam Craig Parore
Born: 23/01/71   Auckland, New Zealand
Country: New Zealand
Right-hand middle order batsman - Wicket-Keeper
Test debut: 05/07/90 v England - Edgbaston, Birmingham

Test Career Record: *Batting & Fielding*									
Mat	Inns	N/O	Runs	H/S	Avg	100s	50s	Cat	St
17	30	4	649	100*	24.96	1	2	43	2

Overseas tours: Eng 90, 94, Pak 90/91, Zim 92/93, SL 92/93, Ind 94/95, SA 94/95, Sharjah 93/94, RW: Eng 92

Test matches: Eng 90 (1), Eng 91/92 (1), Zim 92/93 (2), SL 92/93 (2), Pak 92/93 (1), Aus 92/93 (1), Ind 93/94 (1), Eng 94 (3), SA 94/95 (3), WI 94/95 (2)

Highest score against each country:			100s	50s
Australia	6	Christchurch 92/93	0	0
England	71	Old Trafford 94	0	1
India	17	Hamilton 93/94	0	0
Pakistan	16	Hamilton 92/93	0	0
South Africa	49	Johannesburg 94/95	0	0
Sri Lanka	60	Colombo 92/93	0	1
West Indies	100*	Christchurch 94/95	1	0
Zimbabwe	12	Bulawayo 92/93	0	0

Coopers & Lybrand world rating (batting): 56 (441)

MANOJ PRABHAKAR

Full name: Manoj Prabhakar
Born: 15/04/63   Ghaziabad, India
Country: India
Right-arm medium bowler - Right-hand opening/middle order batsman
Test debut: 12/12/84 v England - Feroz Shah Kotla, Delhi

Test Career Record: *Batting & Fielding*

Mat	Inns	N/O	Runs	H/S	Avg	100s	50s	Cat
36	54	8	1490	120	32.39	1	9	19

Test Career Record: *Bowling*

Balls	Runs	Wkts	Avg	Best	5WI	10WM	BPW
7349	3533	94	37.58	6-132	3	0	78.18

Overseas tours: Eng 86, 90, Pak 89/90, NZ 89/90, 93/94, 94/95, Aus 91/92, Zim 92/93, SA 92/93, SL 93/94, 94/95, Sharjah 83/84, 86/87, 89/90, 91/92, WC: Aus & NZ 91/92, Young Ind: Zim 83/84

Test matches: Eng 84/85 (2), Pak 89/90 (4), NZ 89/90 (3), Eng 90 (3), SL 90/91 (1), Aus 91/92 (5), Zim 92/93 (1), SA 92/93 (4), Eng 92/93 (3), Zim 92/93 (1), SL 93/94 (3), SL 93/94 (3), WI 94/95 (3)

Best bowling against each country:			5WI	10WM
Australia	5-101	Perth 91/92	1	0
England	4-74	The Oval 90	0	0
New Zealand	3-123	Auckland 89/90	0	0
Pakistan	6-132	Faisalabad 89/90	2	0
South Africa	4-90	Johannesburg 92/93	0	0
Sri Lanka	4-82	Bangalore 93/94	0	0
West Indies	2-17	Bombay 94/95	0	0
Zimbabwe	3-66	Harare 92/93	0	0

Coopers & Lybrand world rating (bowling): 20 (523)

Player Profiles

CHRIS PRINGLE

Full name: Christopher Pringle
Born: 26/01/68   Auckland, New Zealand
Country: New Zealand
Right-arm fast medium bowler - Right-hand lower order batsman
Test debut: 10/10/90 v Pakistan - National Stadium, Karachi

Test Career Record: *Batting & Fielding*								
Mat	Inns	N/O	Runs	H/S	Avg	100s	50s	Cat
13	20	4	171	30	10.68	0	0	3
Test Career Record: *Bowling*								
Balls	Runs	Wkts	Avg	Best	5WI	10WM		BPW
2763	1283	27	47.51	7-52	1	1		102.33

Overseas tours: Eng 90, 94, Pak 90/91, Aus 90/91, 93/94, SL 92/93, Ind 94/95, SA 94/95, Sharjah 93/94, RW: Eng 90, 92

Test matches: Pak 90/91 (3), SL 90/91 (2), Eng 91/92 (1), SL 92/93 (1), Pak 93/94 (1), Ind 93/94 (1), Eng 94 (2), SA 94/95 (2)

Best bowling against each country:			5WI	10WM
England	3-127	Christchurch 91/92	0	0
India	2-52	Hamilton 93/94	0	0
Pakistan	7-52	Faisalabad 90/91	1	1
South Africa	1-69	Cape Town 94/95	0	0
Sri Lanka	2-64	Hamilton 90/91	0	0

Coopers & Lybrand world rating (bowling): 68 (190*)

MARK RAMPRAKASH

Full name: Mark Ravin Ramprakash
Born: 05/09/69   Bushey, Hertfordshire, England
Country: England
Right-hand middle order batsman - Off break bowler
Test debut: 06/06/91 v West Indies - Headingley, Leeds

Test Career Record: Batting & Fielding								
Mat	Inns	N/O	Runs	H/S	Avg	100s	50s	Cat
15	26	1	498	72	19.92	0	2	11

Test Career Record: Bowling							
Balls	Runs	Wkts	Avg	Best	5WI	10WM	BPW
241	130	0	-	-	-	-	-

Overseas tours: NZ 91/92, WI 93/94, Aus 94/95, Eng A: Pak & SL 90/91, WI 91/92, Ind & Ban 94/95

Test matches: WI 91 (5), SL 91 (1), Pak 92 (3), Aus 93 (1), WI 93/94 (4), Aus 94/95 (1)

Highest score against each country:			100s	50s
Australia	72	Perth 94/95	0	2
Pakistan	17	The Oval 92	0	0
Sri Lanka	0	Lord's 91	0	0
West Indies	29	Edgbaston 91	0	0

Coopers & Lybrand world rating (batting): 67 (367)

Player Profiles

ARJUNA RANATUNGA

Full name: Arjuna Ranatunga
Born: 01/12/63   Colombo, Sri Lanka
Country: Sri Lanka
Left-hand middle order batsman - Right-arm medium bowler
Test debut: 17/02/82 v England - Saravanamuttu Stadium, Colombo

Test Career Record: *Batting & Fielding*								
Mat	Inns	N/O	Runs	H/S	Avg	100s	50s	Cat
54	90	5	2961	135*	34.83	4	18	22

Test Career Record: *Bowling*							
Balls	Runs	Wkts	Avg	Best	5WI	10WM	BPW
2162	942	14	67.28	2-17	0	0	154.42

Overseas tours: Pak 81/82, 85/86, 91/92, Zim 82/83, 94/95, Ind 82/83, 86/87, 89/90, 90/91, 93/94, Eng 84, 88, Aus 84/85, 87/88, 89/90, NZ 90/91, SA 94/95, Ban 88/89, Sharjah 83/84, 85/86, 86/87, 87/88, 88/89, 89/90, 90/91, 92/93, 93/94, WC: Eng 83, Ind & Pak 87/88, Aus & NZ 91/92, SL under 23: Pak 83/84

Test matches: Eng 81/82 (1), Pak 81/82 (2), Ind 82/83 (1), Aus 82/83 (1), NZ 83/84 (3), Eng 84 (1), Ind 85/86 (3), Pak 85/86 (3), Pak 85/86 (3), Ind 86/87 (3), NZ 86/87 (1), Aus 87/88 (1), Eng 88 (1), Aus 89/90 (2), Ind 90/91 (1), NZ 90/91 (3), Pak 91/92 (3), Aus 92/93 (3), NZ 92/93 (2), Eng 92/93 (1), Ind 93/94 (3), SA 93/94 (3), WI 93/94 (1), Ind 93/94 (3), Pak 94/95 (2), Zim 94/95 (3)

The Test Cricketer's Almanac

Highest score against each country:			100s	50s
Australia	127	Colombo 92/93	1	2
England	84	Lord's 84	0	4
India	111	Colombo 85/86	1	3
New Zealand	76	Colombo 92/93	0	4
Pakistan	135*	Colombo 85/86	1	3
South Africa	131	Moratuwa 93/94	1	1
West Indies	31	Moratuwa 93/94	0	0
Zimbabwe	62	Harare 94/95	0	1

Coopers & Lybrand world rating (batting): 40 (517)

Player Profiles

RASHID LATIF

Full name: Rashid Latif
Born: 14/10/68   Karachi, Pakistan
Country: Pakistan
Right-hand middle order batsman - Wicket-Keeper - Leg break bowler
Test debut: 06/08/92 v England - The Oval, London

Test Career Record: *Batting & Fielding*									
Mat	Inns	N/O	Runs	H/S	Avg	100s	50s	Cat	St
16	24	4	535	68*	26.75	0	3	44	5

Test Career Record: *Bowling*							
Balls	Runs	Wkts	Avg	Best	5WI	10WM	BPW
12	11	0	-	-	-	-	-

Overseas tours: Eng 92, Aus 92/93, NZ 92/93, 93/94, SA 92/93, 94/95, WI 92/93, Zim 92/93, 94/95, SL 94/95, Sharjah 92/93, 93/94

Test matches: Eng 92 (1), NZ 92/93 (1), WI 92/93 (1), Zim 93/94 (3), NZ 93/94 (3), SL 94/95 (2), Aus 94/95 (2), Zim 94/95 (3)

Highest score against each country:			100s	50s
Australia	38	Rawalpindi 94/95	0	0
England	50	The Oval 92	0	1
New Zealand	33	Hamilton 92/93	0	0
Sri Lanka	7	Kandy 94/95	0	0
West Indies	4	St John's 92/93	0	0
Zimbabwe	68 *	Karachi 93/94	0	2

Coopers & Lybrand world rating (batting): 64 (378)

PAUL REIFFEL

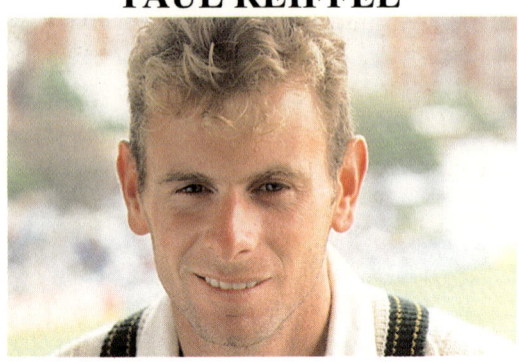

Full name: Paul Ronald Reiffel
Born: 19/04/66   Box Hill, Melbourne, Victoria, Australia
Country: Australia
Right-arm fast medium bowler - Right-hand lower order batsman
Test debut: 01/02/92 v India - WACA Ground, Perth

Test Career Record: *Batting & Fielding*								
Mat	Inns	N/O	Runs	H/S	Avg	100s	50s	Cat
12	13	3	227	51	22.70	0	1	5
Test Career Record: *Bowling*								
Balls	Runs	Wkts	Avg	Best	5WI	10WM		BPW
2380	1050	31	33.87	6-71	2	0		76.77

Overseas tours: NZ 92/93, 94/95, Eng 93, SA 93/94, WI 94/95, Sharjah 93/94, Aus B: Zim 91/92

Test matches: Ind 91/92 (1), NZ 92/93 (3), Eng 93 (3), NZ 93/94 (2), SA 93/94 (2), SA 93/94 (1)

Best bowling against each country:			5WI	10WM
England	6-71	Edgbaston 93	2	0
India	2-34	Perth 91/92	0	0
New Zealand	2-27	Christchurch 92/93	0	0
South Africa	2-77	Durban 93/94	0	0

Coopers & Lybrand world rating (bowler): 26 (446*)

Player Profiles

'JONTY' RHODES

Full name: Jonathan Neil Rhodes
Born: 26/07/69   Pietermaritzburg, South Africa
Country: South Africa
Right-hand middle order batsman
Test debut: 13/11/92 v India - Kingsmead, Durban

Test Career Record: *Batting & Fielding*								
Mat	Inns	N/O	Runs	H/S	Avg	100s	50s	Cat
20	33	5	1009	101*	36.03	1	6	1
Test Career Record: *Bowling*								
Balls	Runs	Wkts	Avg	Best	5WI	10WM	BPW	
12	5	0	-	-	-	-	-	

Overseas tours: WI 91/92, SL 93/94, Ind 93/94, Aus 93/94, Eng 94, Pak 94/95, NZ 94/95, WC: Aus & NZ 91/92

Test matches: Ind 92/93 (4), SL 93/94 (3), Aus 93/94 (3), Aus 93/94 (3), Eng 94 (3), NZ 94/95 (3), Pak 94/95 (1)

Highest score against each country:			100s	50s
Australia	78	Durban 93/94	0	3
England	46	Headingley 94	0	0
India	91	Johannesburg 92/93	0	2
New Zealand	37	Johannesburg 94/95	0	0
Pakistan	72	Johannesburg 94/95	0	1
Sri Lanka	101*	Moratuwa 93/94	1	0

Coopers & Lybrand world rating (batting): 37 (536)

STEVE RHODES

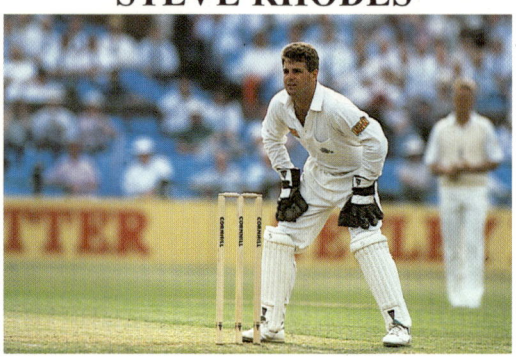

Full name: Steven John Rhodes
Born: 17/06/64   Dirkhill, Bradford, Yorkshire, England
Country: England
Right-hand middle order batsman - Wicket-Keeper
Test debut: 02/06/94 v New Zealand - Trent Bridge, Nottingham

Test Career Record: *Batting & Fielding*									
Mat	Inns	N/O	Runs	H/S	Avg	100s	50s	Cat	St
11	17	5	294	65*	24.50	0	1	46	3

Overseas tours: Aus 94/95, Eng A: Zim & Ken 89/90, Pak & SL 90/91, WI 91/92, SA 93/94, Eng B: SL 85/86

Test matches: NZ 94 (3), SA 94 (3), Aus 94/95 (5)

Highest score against each country:			100s	50s
Australia	39*	Perth 94/95	0	0
New Zealand	49	Trent Bridge 94	0	0
South Africa	65*	Headingley 94	0	1

Coopers & Lybrand world rating (batting): 92= (252*)

DAVID RICHARDSON

Full name: David John Richardson
Born: 16/09/59   Johannesburg, South Africa
Country: South Africa
Right-hand middle order batsman - Wicket-Keeper
Test debut: 18/04/92 v West Indies - Kensington Oval, Bridgetown

Test Career Record: *Batting & Fielding*									
Mat	Inns	N/O	Runs	H/S	Avg	100s	50s	Cat	St
21	32	2	799	109	26.63	1	5	85	0

Overseas tours: Ind 91/92, 93/94, WI 91/92, SL 93/94, Aus 93/94, Eng 94, Pak 94/95, NZ 94/95, WC: Aus & NZ 91/92

Test matches: WI 91/92 (1), Ind 92/93 (4), SL 93/94 (3), Aus 93/94 (3), Aus 93/94 (3), Eng 94 (3), NZ 94/95 (3), Pak 94/95 (1)

Highest score against each country:			100s	50s
Australia	59	Durban 93/94	0	1
England	58	The Oval 94	0	1
India	50	Johannesburg 92/93	0	1
New Zealand	109	Cape Town 94/95	1	1
Pakistan	0	Johannesburg 94/95	0	0
Sri Lanka	62	Colombo 93/94	0	1
West Indies	8	Bridgetown 91/92	0	0

Coopers & Lybrand world rating (batting): 51 (482)

RICHIE RICHARDSON

Full name: Richard Benjamin Richardson
Born: 12/01/62   Five Islands Village, Antigua
Country: West Indies
Right-hand middle order batsman - Right-arm medium bowler
Test debut: 24/11/83 v India - Wankhede Stadium, Bombay

Test Career Record: *Batting & Fielding*								
Mat	Inns	N/O	Runs	H/S	Avg	100s	50s	Cat
76	130	11	5445	194	45.75	15	25	82
Test Career Record: *Bowling*								
Balls	Runs	Wkts	Avg	Best	5WI	10WM		BPW
66	18	0	-	-	-	-		-

Overseas tours: Ind 83/84, 87/88, 89/90, 93/94, Aus 83/84, 84/85, 86/87, 88/89, 91/92, 92/93, Eng 84, 88, 91, Pak 85/86, 86/87, 90/91, 91/92, NZ 86/87, SA 92/93, SL 93/94, Sharjah 85/86, 86/87, 88/89, 89/90, 91/92, 93/94, WC: Ind & Pak 87/88, Aus & NZ 91/92, RW: Eng 90, 92

Test matches: Ind 83/84 (1), Aus 83/84 (5), Aus 84/85 (5), NZ 84/85 (4), Eng 85/86 (5), Pak 86/87 (3), NZ 86/87 (3), Ind 87/88 (4), Pak 87/88 (3), Eng 88 (3), Aus 88/89 (5), Ind 88/89 (4), Eng 89/90 (4), Pak 90/91 (3), Aus 90/91 (5), Eng 91 (5), SA 91/92 (1), Aus 92/93 (5), Pak 92/93 (3), SL 93/94 (1), Eng 93/94 (4)

Highest score against each country:			100s	50s
Australia	182	Georgetown 90/91	8	7
England	160	Bridgetown 85/86	4	4
India	194	Georgetown 88/89	2	5
New Zealand	185	Georgetown 84/85	1	2
Pakistan	75	Georgetown 87/88	0	6
South Africa	44	Bridgetown 91/92	0	0
Sri Lanka	51	Moratuwa 93/94	0	1

Coopers & Lybrand world rating (batting): 12 (664)

'JACK' RUSSELL

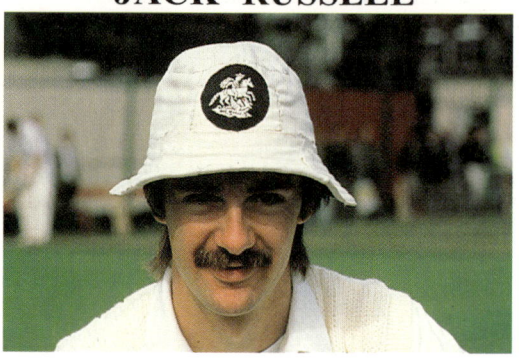

Full name: Robert Charles Russell
Born: 15/08/63 Stroud, Gloucestershire
Country: England
Left-hand middle order batsman - Wicket-Keeper
Test debut: 25/08/88 v Sri Lanka - Lord's, London

Test Career Record: *Batting & Fielding*									
Mat	Inns	N/O	Runs	H/S	Avg	100s	50s	Cat	St
36	58	11	1255	128*	26.70	1	4	90	8

Overseas tours: Pak 87/88, Ind 89/90, WI 89/90, 93/94, Aus 90/91, 94/95, NZ 90/91, 91/92, Eng A: Aus 92/93

Test matches: SL 88 (1), Aus 89 (6), WI 89/90 (4), NZ 90 (3), Ind 90 (3), Aus 90/91 (3), WI 91 (4), SL 91 (1), NZ 91/92 (3), Pak 92 (3), WI 93/94 (5)

Highest score against each country:			100s	50s
Australia	128*	Old Trafford 89	1	1
India	35	The Oval 90	0	0
New Zealand	43	Edgbaston 90	0	0
Pakistan	29*	Edgbaston 92	0	0
Sri Lanka	94	Lord's 88	0	1
West Indies	62	St John's 93/94	0	2

Coopers & Lybrand world rating (batting): 73 (309)

KEN RUTHERFORD

Full name: Kenneth Robert Rutherford
Born: 26/10/65   Dunedin, New Zealand
Country: New Zealand
Right-hand middle order batsman - Right-arm medium bowler
Test debut: 29/03/85 v West Indies - Queens Park Oval, Port of Spain

Test Career Record: *Batting & Fielding*								
Mat	Inns	N/O	Runs	H/S	Avg	100s	50s	Cat
53	95	8	2329	107*	26.77	3	17	30
Test Career Record: *Bowling*							
Balls	Runs	Wkts	Avg	Best	5WI	10WM	BPW
256	161	1	161.00	1-38	0	0	256.00

Overseas tours: WI 84/85, SL 85/86, 86/87, 92/93, Eng 86, 90, 94, Aus 87/88, 90/91, 93/94, Ind 88/89, 94/95, Pak 90/91, Zim 92/93, SA 94/95, Sharjah 85/86, 87/88, 89/90, WC: Ind 87/88, Young NZ: Zim 84/85, 88/89

Test matches: WI 84/85 (4), Aus 85/86 (3), Eng 86 (1), WI 86/87 (2), SL 86/87 (1), Aus 87/88 (1), Eng 87/88 (2), Ind 88/89 (2), Ind 89/90 (3), Aus 89/90 (1), Eng 90 (2), Pak 90/91 (3), SL 90/91 (3), Eng 91/92 (2), Zim 92/93 (2), SL 92/93 (2), Pak 92/93 (1), Aus 92/93 (3), Aus 93/94 (3), Pak 93/94 (3), Ind 93/94 (1), Eng 94 (3), SA 94/95 (3), WI 94/95 (2)

Highest score against each country:			100s	50s
Australia	102	Christchurch 92/93	1	6
England	107*	Wellington 87/88	1	0
India	69	Christchurch 89/90	0	3
Pakistan	79	Karachi 90/91	0	3
South Africa	68	Johannesburg 94/95	0	2
Sri Lanka	105	Moratuwa 92/93	1	1
West Indies	22	Wellington 94/95	0	0
Zimbabwe	89	Harare 92/93	0	2

Coopers & Lybrand world rating (batting): 54 (459)

Player Profiles

SALIM MALIK

Full name: Salim Malik
Born: 16/04/63   Lahore, Pakistan
Country: Pakistan
Right-hand middle order batsman - Right-arm medium or leg break bowler
Test debut: 05/03/82 v Sri Lanka - National Stadium, Karachi

Test Career Record: *Batting & Fielding*								
Mat	Inns	N/O	Runs	H/S	Avg	100s	50s	Cat
84	124	19	4804	237	45.75	13	24	54

Test Career Record: *Bowling*							
Balls	Runs	Wkts	Avg	Best	5WI	10WM	BPW
422	246	5	49.20	1-3	0	0	84.40

Overseas tours: Aus 81/82, 83/84, 84/85, 88/89, 89/90, 91/92, 92/93, Eng 82, 87, 92, Ind 83/84, 86/87, 89/90, NZ 84/85, 88/89, 92/93, 93/94, SL 85/86, 94/95, WI 87/88, SA 92/93, 94/95, Zim 94/95, Ban 88/89, Sharjah 83/84, 84/85, 85/86, 86/87, 88/89, 89/90, 90/91, 91/92, 92/93, 93/94, WC: Aus & NZ 91/92, Pak under 23: SL 84/85

Test matches: SL 81/82 (2), Ind 82/83 (6), Ind 83/84 (2), Aus 83/84 (3), Eng 83/84 (3), Ind 84/85 (2), NZ 84/85 (3), NZ 84/85 (3), SL 85/86 (3), SL 85/86 (3), WI 86/87 (1), Ind 86/87 (5), Eng 87 (5), Eng 87/88 (3), WI 87/88 (3), Aus 88/89 (3), NZ 88/89 (2), Ind 89/90 (4), Aus 89/90 (1), NZ 90/91 (3), WI 90/91 (3), SL 91/92 (3), Eng 92 (5), NZ 92/93 (1), NZ 93/94 (3), SL 94/95 (2), Aus 94/95 (3), SA 94/95 (1), Zim 94/95 (3)

Highest score against each country:			100s	50s
Australia	237	Rawalpindi 94/95	2	4
England	165	Edgbaston 92	3	8
India	107	Faisalabad 82/83	3	2
New Zealand	140	Wellington 93/94	2	4
South Africa	99	Johannesburg 94/95	0	1
Sri Lanka	101	Sialkot 91/92	2	2
West Indies	102	Karachi 90/91	1	3
Zimbabwe	44	Bulawayo 94/95	0	0

Coopers & Lybrand world rating (batting): 8 (708)

Player Profiles

IAN SALISBURY

Full name: Ian David Kenneth Salisbury
Born: 21/01/70   Northampton, England
Country: England
Leg break and googly bowler - Right-hand lower order batsman
Test debut: 18/06/92 v Pakistan - Lord's, London

Test Career Record: *Batting & Fielding*								
Mat	Inns	N/O	Runs	H/S	Avg	100s	50s	Cat
7	13	1	205	50	17.08	0	1	3

Test Career Record: *Bowling*							
Balls	Runs	Wkts	Avg	Best	5WI	10WM	BPW
1405	933	16	58.31	4-163	0	0	87.81

Overseas tours: Ind 92/93, SL 92/93, WI 93/94, Eng A: Pak & SL 90/91, WI 91/92, Ind & Ban 94/95

Test matches: Pak 92 (2), Ind 92/93 (2), WI 93/94 (2), SA 94 (1)

Best bowling against each country:			5WI	10WM
India	2-142	Madras 92/93	0	0
Pakistan	3-49	Lord's 92	0	0
South Africa	1-53	Lord's 94	0	0
West Indies	4-163	Georgetown 93/94	0	0

Coopers & Lybrand world rating (bowling): 81 (94*)

NAVJOT SIDHU

Full name: Navjot Singh Sidhu
Born: 20/10/63   Patiala, India
Country: India
Right-hand opening batsman
Test debut: 12/11/83 v West Indies - Gujarat Stadium, Ahmedabad

Test Career Record: Batting & Fielding								
Mat	Inns	N/O	Runs	H/S	Avg	100s	50s	Cat
34	52	2	2013	124	40.26	6	10	8

Test Career Record: Bowling							
Balls	Runs	Wkts	Avg	Best	5WI	10WM	BPW
6	9	0	-	-	-	-	-

Overseas tours: WI 88/89, Pak 89/90, NZ 89/90, 93/94, 94/95, Eng 90, Aus 91/92, SL 93/94, 94/95, Ban 88/89, Sharjah 87/88, 88/89, 89/90, 91/92, 93/94

Test matches: WI 83/84 (2), NZ 88/89 (3), WI 88/89 (4), Pak 89/90 (4), NZ 89/90 (1), Eng 90 (3), Aus 91/92 (3), Eng 92/93 (3), Zim 92/93 (1), SL 93/94 (3), SL 93/94 (3), NZ 93/94 (1), WI 94/95 (3)

Highest score against each country:			100s	50s
Australia	35	Adelaide 91/92	0	0
	35	Perth 91/92		
England	106	Madras 92/93	1	1
New Zealand	116	Bangalore 88/89	1	2
Pakistan	97	Sialkot 89/90	0	3
Sri Lanka	124	Lucknow 93/94	2	2
West Indies	116	Kingston 88/89	2	1
Zimbabwe	61	Delhi 92/93	0	1

Coopers & Lybrand world rating (batting): 23= (603)

Player Profiles

PHIL SIMMONS

Full name: Philip Verant Simmons
Born: 18/04/63   Arima, Trinidad
Country: West indies
Right-hand opening batsman - Right-arm medium bowler
Test debut: 11/01/88 v India - Chidambaram Stadium, Chepauk, Madras

\multicolumn{9}{l}{**Test Career Record:** *Batting & Fielding*}

Test Career Record: *Batting & Fielding*

Mat	Inns	N/O	Runs	H/S	Avg	100s	50s	Cat
22	41	2	919	110	23.56	1	3	21

Test Career Record: *Bowling*

Balls	Runs	Wkts	Avg	Best	5WI	10WM	BPW
396	158	2	79.00	2-34	0	0	198.00

Overseas tours: Ind 87/88, 89/90, 93/94, 94/95, Eng 88, 91, Aus 92/93, SA 92/93, SL 93/94, Sharjah 89/90, 91/92, 93/94, WC: Pak & Ind 87/88, Aus & NZ 91/92, Young WI: Zim 86/87, RW: Eng 92, 93

Test matches: Ind 87/88 (1), Pak 87/88 (1), Eng 91 (5), SA 91/92 (1), Aus 92/93 (5), Pak 92/93 (3), SL 93/94 (1), Eng 93/94 (2), Ind 94/95 (3)

Highest score against each country:			100s	50s
Australia	110	Melbourne 92/93	1	1
England	38	Headingley 91	0	0
India	50	Nagpur 94/95	0	1
Pakistan	87	Bridgetown 92/93	0	1
South Africa	35	Bridgetown 91/92	0	0
Sri Lanka	17	Moratuwa 93/94	0	0

Coopers & Lybrand world rating (batting): 61 (423)

The Test Cricketer's Almanac

MICHAEL SLATER

Full name: Michael Jonathon Slater
Born: 21/02/70   Wagga Wagga, New South Wales, Australia
Country: Australia
Right-hand opening batsman
Test debut: 03/06/93 v England - Old Trafford, Manchester

Test Career Record: *Batting & Fielding*								
Mat	Inns	N/O	Runs	H/S	Avg	100s	50s	Cat
23	40	1	2024	176	51.89	6	8	4
Test Career Record: *Bowling*								
Balls	Runs	Wkts	Avg	Best	5WI	10WM		BPW
7	4	1	4.00	1-4	0	0		7.00

Overseas tours: Eng 93, SA 93/94, SL 94/95, Pak 94/95, WI 94/95, Sharjah 93/94

Test matches: Eng 93 (6), NZ 93/94 (3), SA 93/94 (3), SA 93/94 (3), Pak 94/95 (3), Eng 94/95 (5)

Highest score against each country:			100s	50s
England	176	Brisbane 94/95	4	3
New Zealand	168	Hobart 93/94	1	1
Pakistan	110	Rawalpindi 94/95	1	1
South Africa	95	Durban 93/94	0	3

Coopers & Lybrand world rating (batting): 7 (755)

Player Profiles

ROBIN SMITH

Full name: Robin Arnold Smith
Born: 13/09/63   Durban, South Africa
Country: England
Right-hand middle order batsman - Off break bowler
Test debut: 21/07/88 v West Indies - Headingley, Leeds

Test Career Record: *Batting & Fielding*								
Mat	Inns	N/O	Runs	H/S	Avg	100s	50s	Cat
53	97	14	3677	175	44.30	9	24	35
Test Career Record: *Bowling*								
Balls	Runs	Wkts	Avg	Best	5WI	10WM	BPW	
24	6	0	-	-	-	-	-	

Overseas tours: Ind 89/90, 92/93, WI 89/90, 93/94, Aus 90/91, NZ 90/91, 91/92, SL 92/93, WC: Aus & NZ 91/92

Test matches: WI 88 (2), SL 88 (1), Aus 89 (5), WI 89/90 (4), NZ 90 (3), Ind 90 (3), Aus 90/91 (5), WI 91 (4), SL 91 (1), NZ 91/92 (3), Pak 92 (5), Ind 92/93 (3), SL 92/93 (1), Aus 93 (5), WI 93/94 (5), NZ 94 (3)

Highest score against each country:			100s	50s
Australia	143	Old Trafford 89	2	7
India	121*	Old Trafford 90	2	4
New Zealand	96	Christchurch 91/92	0	5
Pakistan	127	Edgbaston 92	1	1
Sri Lanka	128	Colombo 92/93	1	1
West Indies	175	St John's 93/94	3	6

Coopers & Lybrand world rating (batting): 43 (508)

RICHARD SNELL

Full name: Richard Peter Snell
Born: 12/09/68   Durban, South Africa
Country: South Africa
Right-arm fast medium bowler - Right-hand lower order batsman
Test debut: 18/04/92 v West Indies - Kensington Oval, Bridgetown

Test Career Record: *Batting & Fielding*								
Mat	Inns	N/O	Runs	H/S	Avg	100s	50s	Cat
5	8	1	95	48	13.57	0	0	1

Test Career Record: *Bowling*							
Balls	Runs	Wkts	Avg	Best	5WI	10WM	BPW
1025	539	19	28.36	4-74	0	0	53.94

Overseas tours: Ind 91/92, 93/94, WI 91/92, SL 93/94, Aus 93/94, Eng 94, WC: Aus & NZ 91/92

Test matches: WI 91/92 (1), SL 93/94 (2), Aus 93/94 (1), NZ 94/95 (1)

Best bowling against each country:			5WI	10WM
Australia	2-38	Adelaide 93/94	0	0
New Zealand	3-112	Johannesburg 94/95	0	0
Sri Lanka	3-32	Colombo 93/94	0	0
West Indies	4-74	Bridgetown 91/92	0	0

Coopers & Lybrand world rating (bowling): 51 (263*)

Player Profiles

JAVAGAL SRINATH

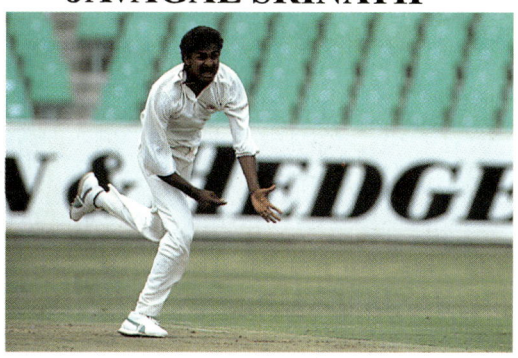

Full name: Javagal Srinath
Born: 31/08/69   Mysore, India
Country: India
Right-arm fast medium bowler - Right-hand middle order batsman
Test debut: 29/11/91 v Australia - Woolloongabba, Brisbane

Test Career Record: *Batting & Fielding*

Mat	Inns	N/O	Runs	H/S	Avg	100s	50s	Cat
15	21	11	227	60	22.70	0	2	7

Test Career Record: *Bowling*

Balls	Runs	Wkts	Avg	Best	5WI	10WM	BPW
3522	1549	41	37.78	4-33	0	0	85.90

Overseas tours: Aus 91/92, Zim 92/93, SA 92/93, SL 93/94, 94/95, NZ 93/94, 94/95, Sharjah 91/92, 93/94

Test matches: Aus 91/92 (5), Zim 92/93 (1), SA 92/93 (3), SL 93/94 (2), NZ 93/94 (1), WI 94/95 (3)

Best bowling against each country:			5WI	10WM
Australia	3-59	Brisbane 91/92	0	0
New Zealand	4-60	Hamilton 93/94	0	0
South Africa	4-33	Cape Town 92/93	0	0
Sri Lanka	2-42	Colombo 93/94	0	0
West Indies	4-48	Bombay 94/95	0	0
Zimbabwe	3-89	Harare 92/93	0	0

Coopers & Lybrand world rating (bowling): 29 (406*)

ALEC STEWART

Full name: Alec James Stewart
Born: 08/04/63 Merton, Surrey, England
Country: England
Right-hand opening/middle order batsman - Wicket-Keeper
Test debut: 24/02/90 v West Indies - Sabina Park, Kingston

Test Career Record: *Batting & Fielding*									
Mat	Inns	N/O	Runs	H/S	Avg	100s	50s	Cat	St
45	82	6	3055	190	40.19	7	15	55	4
Test Career Record: *Bowling*									
Balls	Runs	Wkts	Avg	Best	5WI	10WM			BPW
20	13	0	-	-	-	-			-

Overseas tours: Ind 89/90, 92/93, WI 89/90, 93/94, Aus 90/91, 94/95, NZ 90/91, 91/92, SL 92/93, WC: Aus & NZ 91/92

Test matches: WI 89/90 (4), NZ 90 (3), Aus 90/91 (5), WI 91 (1), SL 91 (1), NZ 91/92 (3), Pak 92 (5), Ind 92/93 (3), SL 92/93 (1), Aus 93 (6), WI 93/94 (5), NZ 94 (3), SA 94 (3), Aus 94/95 (2)

Highest score against each country:			100s	50s
Australia	91	Sydney 90/91	0	5
India	74	Madras 92/93	0	1
New Zealand	148	Christchurch 91/92	3	2
Pakistan	190	Edgbaston 92	1	2
South Africa	89	Headingley 94	0	2
Sri Lanka	113*	Lord's 91	1	1
West Indies	143	Bridgetown 93/94	2	2

Coopers & Lybrand world rating (batting): 13 (659)

HEATH STREAK

Full name: Heath Hilton Streak
Born: 16/03/74   Bulawayo, Zimbabwe
Country: Zimbabwe
Right-arm medium bowler - Right-hand lower order batsman
Test debut: 01/12/93 v Pakistan - Defence Stadium, Karachi

Test Career Record: Batting & Fielding								
Mat	*Inns*	*N/O*	*Runs*	*H/S*	*Avg*	*100s*	*50s*	*Cat*
9	12	2	103	30*	10.30	0	0	3
Test Career Record: Bowling								
Balls	*Runs*	*Wkts*		*Avg*	*Best*	*5WI*	*10WM*	*BPW*
2182	886	43		20.60	6-90	3	0	50.74

Overseas tours: Eng 93, Ind 93/94, Pak 93/94, Aus 94/95

Test matches: Pak 93/94 (3), SL 94/95 (3), Pak 94/95 (3)

Best bowling against each country:			**5WI**	**10WM**
Pakistan	6-90	Harare 94/95	3	0
Sri Lanka	4-79	Harare 94/95	0	0

Coopers & Lybrand world rating (bowling): 4 (819*)

The Test Cricketer's Almanac

MARK TAYLOR

Full name: Mark Anthony Taylor
Born: 27/10/64   Leeton, New South Wales, Australia
Country: Australia
Left-hand opening batsman - Right-arm medium bowler
Test debut: 26/01/89 v West Indies - Sydney C. G.

Test Career Record: *Batting & Fielding*								
Mat	Inns	N/O	Runs	H/S	Avg	100s	50s	Cat
62	112	7	4853	219	46.21	13	29	83
Test Career Record: *Bowling*								
Balls	Runs	Wkts	Avg	Best	5WI	10WM	BPW	
42	26	1	26.00	1-11	0	0	42.00	

Overseas tours: Eng 89, 93, NZ 89/90, 92/93, 94/95, WI 90/91, 94/95, SL 92/93, 94/95, SA 93/94, Pak 94/95, Sharjah 89/90, 93/94, Aus B: Zim 91/92

Test matches: WI 88/89 (2), Eng 89 (6), NZ 89/90 (1), SL 89/90 (2), Pak 89/90 (3), NZ 89/90 (1), Eng 90/91 (5), WI 90/91 (5), Ind 91/92 (5), SL 92/93 (3), WI 92/93 (4), NZ 92/93 (3), Eng 93 (6), NZ 93/94 (3), SA 93/94 (3), SA 93/94 (2), Pak 94/95 (3), Eng 94/95 (5)

Highest score against each country:			100s	50s
England	219	Trent Bridge 89	5	12
India	100	Adelaide 91/92	1	3
New Zealand	142 *	Perth 93/94	1	4
Pakistan	101 *	Sydney 89/90	2	4
	101	Melbourne 89/90		
South Africa	170	Melbourne 93/94	1	2
Sri Lanka	164	Brisbane 89/90	2	0
West Indies	144	St John's 90/91	1	4

Coopers & Lybrand world rating (batting): 21 (613)

Player Profiles

SACHIN TENDULKAR

Full name: Sachin Ramesh Tendulkar
Born: 24/04/73   Bombay, India
Country: India
Right-hand middle order batsman - Right-arm medium bowler
Test debut: 15/11/89 v Pakistan - National Stadium, Karachi

Test Career Record: *Batting & Fielding*								
Mat	Inns	N/O	Runs	H/S	Avg	100s	50s	Cat
35	51	5	2425	179	52.71	8	12	28

Test Career Record: *Bowling*							
Balls	Runs	Wkts	Avg	Best	5WI	10WM	BPW
432	191	4	47.75	2-10	0	0	108.00

Overseas tours: Pak 89/90, NZ 89/90, 93/94, 94/95, Eng 90, Aus 91/92, Zim 92/93, SA 92/93, SL 93/94, 94/95, Sharjah 89/90, 91/92, 93/94, WC: Aus & NZ 91/92, RW: Eng 91

Test matches: Pak 89/90 (4), NZ 89/90 (3), Eng 90 (3), SL 90/91 (1), Aus 91/92 (5), Zim 92/93 (1), SA 92/93 (4), Eng 92/93 (3), Zim 92/93 (1), SL 93/94 (3), SL 93/94 (3), NZ 93/94 (1), WI 94/95 (3)

Highest score against each country:			100s	50s
Australia	148*	Sydney 91/92	2	0
England	165	Madras 92/93	2	3
New Zealand	88	Napier 89/90	0	1
Pakistan	59	Faisalabad 89/90	0	2
South Africa	111	Johannesburg 92/93	1	1
Sri Lanka	142	Lucknow 93/94	2	2
West Indies	179	Nagpur 94/95	1	2
Zimbabwe	62	Delhi 92/93	0	1

Coopers & Lybrand world rating (batting): 4 (774)

SHANE THOMSON

Full name: Shane Alexander Thomson
Born: 27/01/69   Hamilton, Auckland, New Zealand
Country: New Zealand
Right-hand middle order batsman - Right-arm fast medium bowler
Test debut: 22/02/90 v India - Eden Park, Auckland

Test Career Record: *Batting & Fielding*								
Mat	Inns	N/O	Runs	H/S	Avg	100s	50s	Cat
16	31	4	923	120*	34.18	1	5	7
Test Career Record: *Bowling*								
Balls	Runs	Wkts	Avg	Best	5WI	10WM		BPW
1762	846	19	44.52	3-63	-	-		92.73

Overseas tours: Eng 90, 94, Aus 93/94, Ind 94/95, SA 94/95, Sharjah 89/90, 93/94, Young NZ: Zim 88/89

Test matches: Ind 89/90 (1), SL 90/91 (2), Eng 91/92 (1), Pak 93/94 (3), Ind 93/94 (1), Eng 94 (3), SA 94/95 (3), WI 94/95 (2)

Highest score against each country:			100s	50s
England	69	Lord's 94	0	1
India	43*	Auckland 89/90	0	0
Pakistan	120*	Christchurch 93/94	1	0
South Africa	84	Johannesburg 94/95	0	2
Sri Lanka	80*	Auckland 90/91	0	2
West Indies	20	Christchurch 94/95	0	0

Coopers & Lybrand world rating (batting): 48 (495)

Player Profiles

GRAHAM THORPE

Full name: Graham Paul Thorpe
Born: 01/08/69   Farnham, Surrey, England
Country: England
Left-hand middle order batsman - Right-arm medium bowler
Test debut: 01/07/93 v Australia - Trent Bridge, Nottingham

Test Career Record: *Batting & Fielding*								
Mat	Inns	N/O	Runs	H/S	Avg	100s	50s	Cat
15	29	3	1152	123	44.30	2	9	19
Test Career Record: *Bowling*								
Balls	Runs	Wkts	Avg	Best	5WI	10WM		BPW
48	15	0	-	-	-	-		-

Overseas tours: WI 93/94, Aus 94/95, Eng A: Zim & Ken 89/90, Pak & SL 90/91, WI 91/92, Aus 92/93

Test matches: Aus 93 (3), WI 93/94 (5), SA 94 (2), Aus 94/95 (5)

Highest score against each country:			100s	50s
Australia	123	Perth 94/95	2	4
South Africa	79	The Oval 94	0	3
West Indies	86	Port of Spain 93/94	0	2

Coopers & Lybrand world rating (batting): 5= (758)

HASHAN TILLEKERATNE

Full name: Hashan Prasantha Tillekeratne
Born: 14/07/67   Colombo, Sri Lanka
Country: Sri Lanka
Left-hand middle order batsman - Wicket-Keeper
Test debut: 16/12/89 v Australia - Bellerive Oval, Hobart

Test Career Record: *Batting & Fielding*								
Mat	Inns	N/O	Runs	H/S	Avg	100s	50s	Cat
28	45	7	1413	116	37.18	1	9	62

Test Career Record: *Bowling*							
Balls	Runs	Wkts	Avg	Best	5WI	10WM	BPW
18	6	0	-	-	-	-	-

Overseas tours: Aus 87/88, 89/90, Eng 88, 90, 91, Ind 89/90, 90/91, 93/94, NZ 90/91, Pak 91/92, Zim 94/95, SA 94/95, Ban 88/89, Sharjah 86/87, 88/89, 89/90, 90/91, 92/93, 93/94, WC: Aus & NZ 91/92, SL B: Zim 87/88

Test matches: Aus 89/90 (1), Ind 90/91 (1), NZ 90/91 (3), Eng 91 (1), Pak 91/92 (3), Aus 92/93 (1), NZ 92/93 (2), Eng 92/93 (1), Ind 93/94 (3), SA 93/94 (3), WI 93/94 (1), Ind 93/94 (3), Pak 94/95 (2), Zim 94/95 (3)

Highest score against each country:			100s	50s
Australia	82	Moratuwa 92/93	0	1
England	93 *	Colombo 92/93	0	1
India	86	Colombo 94/93	0	4
New Zealand	93	Colombo 92/93	0	1
Pakistan	83 *	Kandy 94/95	0	1
South Africa	92	Moratuwa 93/94	0	1
West Indies	9 *	Moratuwa 93/94	0	0
Zimbabwe	116	Harare 94/95	1	0

Coopers & Lybrand world rating (batting): 20 (616)

Player Profiles

PHIL TUFNELL

Full name: Philip Clive Roderick Tufnell
Born: 29/04/66   Barnet, Hertfordshire, England
Country: England
Left-arm slow bowler - Right-hand lower order batsman
Test debut: 26/12/90 v Australia - Melbourne Cricket Ground

Test Career Record: *Batting & Fielding*								
Mat	Inns	N/O	Runs	H/S	Avg	100s	50s	Cat
22	32	17	62	22*	4.13	0	0	10
Test Career Record: *Bowling*								
Balls	Runs	Wkts	Avg	Best	5WI	10WM		BPW
6378	2671	68	39.27	7-47	4	1		93.79

Overseas tours: Aus 90/91, 94/95, NZ 90/91, 91/92, Ind 92/93, SL 92/93, WI 93/94, WC: Aus & NZ 91/92

Test matches: Aus 90/91 (4), WI 91 (1), SL 91 (1), NZ 91/92 (3), Pak 92 (1), Ind 92/93 (2), SL 92/93 (1), Aus 93 (2), WI 93/94 (2), SA 94 (1), Aus 94/95 (4)

Best bowling against each country:			5WI	10WM
Australia	5-61	Sydney 90/91	1	0
India	4-142	Bombay 92/93	0	0
New Zealand	7-47	Christchurch 91/92	1	1
Pakistan	1-87	The Oval 92	0	0
South Africa	2-31	Headingley 94	0	0
Sri Lanka	5-94	Lord's 91	1	0
West Indies	6-25	The Oval 91	1	0

Coopers & Lybrand world rating (bowling): 32 (393)

VENKATAPATHY RAJU

Full name: Sagi Lakshmi Venkatapathy Raju
Born: 09/07/69 Hyderabad, India
Country: India
Left-arm slow bowler - Right-hand lower order batsman
Test debut: 02/02/90 v New Zealand - Lancaster Park, Christchurch

Test Career Record: Batting & Fielding								
Mat	Inns	N/O	Runs	H/S	Avg	100s	50s	Cat
21	27	9	228	31	12.66	0	0	5

Test Career Record: Bowling							
Balls	Runs	Wkts	Avg	Best	5WI	10WM	BPW
6158	2273	81	28.06	6-12	5	1	76.02

Overseas tours: NZ 89/90, 93/94, 94/95, Eng 90, Aus 91/92, Zim 92/93, SA 92/93, SL 93/94, 94/95, Sharjah 91/92, 93/94, WC: Aus & NZ 91/92

Test matches: NZ 89/90 (2), SL 90/91 (1), Aus 91/92 (4), Zim 92/93 (1), SA 92/93 (2), Eng 92/93 (3), SL 93/94 (1), SL 93/94 (3), NZ 93/94 (1), WI 94/95 (3)

Best bowling against each country:			5WI	10WM
Australia	3-11	Adelaide 91/92	0	0
England	4-103	Madras 92/93	0	0
New Zealand	3-86	Christchurch 89/90	0	0
South Africa	3-73	Port Elizabeth 92/93	0	0
Sri Lanka	6-12	Chandigarh 90/91	3	1
West Indies	5-60	Bombay 94/95	2	0
Zimbabwe	0-17	Harare 92/93	0	0

Coopers & Lybrand world rating (bowling): 10 (705)

Player Profiles

COURTNEY WALSH

Full name: Courtney Andrew Walsh
Born: 30/10/62   Kingston, Jamaica
Country: West Indies
Right-arm fast bowler - Right-hand lower order batsman
Test debut: 09/11/84 v Australia - WACA Ground, Perth

\multicolumn{9}{l}{**Test Career Record:** *Batting & Fielding*}

Mat	Inns	N/O	Runs	H/S	Avg	100s	50s	Cat
70	93	29	578	30*	9.03	0	0	9

Test Career Record: *Bowling*

Balls	Runs	Wkts	Avg	Best	5WI	10WM	BPW
14455	6317	255	24.77	7-37	9	2	56.68

Overseas tours: Eng 84, 88, 91, Aus 84/85, 86/87, 88/89, 92/93, Pak 85/86, 86/87, 90/91, NZ 86/87, 94/95, Ind 87/88, 89/90, 93/94, 94/95, SA 92/93, SL 93/94, Sharjah 85/86, 86/87, 88/89, 89/90, 91/92, 93/94, WC: Ind & Pak 87/88, Young WI: Zim 83/84, RW: Eng 87

Test matches: Aus 84/85 (5), NZ 84/85 (1), Eng 85/86 (1), Pak 86/87 (3), NZ 86/87 (3), Ind 87/88 (4), Pak 87/88 (3), Eng 88 (5), Aus 88/89 (5), Ind 88/89 (4), Eng 89/90 (3), Pak 90/91 (3), Aus 90/91 (5), Eng 91 (5), SA 91/92 (1), Aus 92/93 (5), Pak 92/93 (3), SL 93/94 (1), Eng 93/94 (5), Ind 94/95 (3), NZ 94/95 (2)

Best bowling against each country:			5WI	10WM
Australia	4-14	Bridgetown 90/91	0	0
England	5-68	Kingston 89/90	2	0
India	6-62	Kingston 88/89	4	1
New Zealand	7-37	Wellington 94/95	3	1
Pakistan	4-21	Lahore 86/87	0	0
South Africa	4-31	Bridgetown 91/92	0	0
Sri Lanka	1-40	Moratuwa 92/93	0	0

Coopers & Lybrand world rating (bowling): 7 (767)

WAQAR YOUNIS

Full name: Waqar Younis
Born: 16/11/71   Vehari, Pakistan
Country: Pakistan
Right-arm fast bowler - Right-hand lower order batsman
Test debut: 15/11/89 v India - National Stadium, Karachi

Test Career Record: *Batting & Fielding*								
Mat	Inns	N/O	Runs	H/S	Avg	100s	50s	Cat
33	41	6	312	29	8.91	0	0	4

Test Career Record: *Bowling*							
Balls	Runs	Wkts	Avg	Best	5WI	10WM	BPW
6858	3641	190	19.16	7-76	19	4	36.09

Overseas tours: Aus 89/90, 92/93, Ind 89/90, WI 91/92, 92/93, Eng 92, NZ 92/93, 93/94, SA 92/93, 94/95, Zim 92/93, SL 94/95, Sharjah 89/90, 90/91, 91/92, 92/93, 93/94

Test Matches: Ind 89/90 (2), Aus 89/90 (3), NZ 90/91 (3), WI 90/91 (3), SL 91/92 (3), Eng 92 (5), NZ 92/93 (1), WI 92/93 (3), Zim 93/94 (3), NZ 93/94 (3), SL 94/95 (2), Aus 94/95 (2)

Best bowling against each country:			5WI	10WM
Australia	4-69	Karachi 94/95	0	0
England	5-52	The Oval 92	3	0
India	4-80	Karachi 89/90	0	0
New Zealand	7-76	Faisalabad 90/91	5	2
Sri Lanka	6-34	Kandy 94/95	4	1
West Indies	5-46	Faisalabad 90/91	3	0
Zimbabwe	7-91	Karachi 93/94	4	1

Coopers & Lybrand world rating (bowling): 3 (859)

Player Profiles

SHANE WARNE

Full name: Shane Keith Warne
Born: 13/09/69 - Ferntree Gully, Melbourne, Victoria, Australia
Country: Australia
Leg break and googly bowler - Right-hand lower order batsman
Test debut: 02/01/92 v India - Sydney Cricket Ground

Test Career Record: *Batting & Fielding*								
Mat	Inns	N/O	Runs	H/S	Avg	100s	50s	Cat
34	48	8	569	74*	14.22	0	1	23

Test Career Record: *Bowling*							
Balls	Runs	Wkts	Avg	Best	5WI	10WM	BPW
10612	3833	161	23.80	8-71	9	2	65.91

Overseas tours: SL 92/93, 94/95, NZ 92/93, 94/95, Eng 93, SA 93/94, Pak 94/95, WI 94/95, Sharjah 93/94, Aus B: Zim 91/92

Test matches: Ind 91/92 (2), SL 92/93 (2), WI 92/93 (4), NZ 92/93 (3), Eng 93 (6), NZ 93/94 (3), SA 93/94 (3), SA 93/94 (3), Pak 94/95 (3), Eng 94/95 (5)

Best bowling against each country:			5WI	10WM
England	8-71	Brisbane 94/95	3	1
India	1-150	Sydney 91/92	0	0
New Zealand	6-31	Hobart 93/94	1	0
Pakistan	6-136	Lahore 94/95	2	0
South Africa	7-56	Sydney 93/94	2	1
Sri Lanka	3-11	Colombo 92/93	0	0
West Indies	7-52	Melbourne 92/93	1	0

Coopers & Lybrand world rating (bowling): 2 (860)

WASIM AKRAM

Full name: Wasim Akram
Born: 03/06/66   Lahore, Pakistan
Country: Pakistan
Left-arm fast bowler - Left-hand middle order batsman
Test debut: 25/01/85 v New Zealand - Eden Park, Auckland

Test Career Record: *Batting & Fielding*								
Mat	Inns	N/O	Runs	H/S	Avg	100s	50s	Cat
61	82	11	1398	123	19.69	1	4	21
Test Career Record: *Bowling*								
Balls	Runs	Wkts	Avg	Best	5WI	10WM		BPW
14039	6057	261	23.20	7-119	18	3		53.78

Overseas tours: Aus 84/85, 86/87, 88/89, 89/90, 91/92, 92/93, NZ 84/85, 88/89, 92/93, 93/94, SL 85/86, 94/95, Ind 86/87, 89/90, Eng 87, 92, WI 87/88, 92/93, SA 92/93, 94/95, Zim 92/93, 94/95, Ban 88/89, Sharjah: 84/85, 85/86, 86/87, 88/89, 89/90, 90/91, 91/92, 92/93, 93/94, 94/95, WC: Aus & NZ 91/92, Pak under 23: SL 84/85

Test matches: NZ 84/85 (2), SL 85/86 (3), SL 85/86 (3), WI 86/87 (2), Ind 86/87 (5), Eng 87 (5), Eng 87/88 (2), WI 87/88 (3), Ind 89/90 (4), Aus 89/90 (3), NZ 90/91 (2), WI 90/91 (3), SL 91/92 (3), Eng 92 (4), NZ 92/93 (1), WI 92/93 (3), Zim 93/94 (2), NZ 93/94 (3), SL 94/95 (2), Aus 94/95 (2), SA 94/95 (1), Zim 94/95 (3)

Best bowling against each country:			5WI	10WM
Australia	6-62	Melbourne 89/90	4	1
England	6-67	The Oval 92	2	0
India	5-96	Calcutta 86/87	2	0
New Zealand	7-119	Wellington 93/94	5	2
South Africa	2-53	Johannesburg 94/95	0	0
Sri Lanka	5-43	Colombo 94/95	1	0
West Indies	6-91	Faisalabad 86/87	2	0
Zimbabwe	5-43	Bulawayo 94/95	2	0

Coopers & Lybrand world rating (bowling): 8 (757)

MARK WAUGH

Full name: Mark Edward Waugh
Born: 02/06/65 Canterbury, Sydney, New South Wales, Australia
Country: Australia
Right-hand middle order batsman - Right-arm medium bowler
Test debut: 25/01/91 v England - Adelaide Oval

Test Career Record: Batting & Fielding								
Mat	Inns	N/O	Runs	H/S	Avg	100s	50s	Cat
44	71	4	2832	140	42.26	7	17	59

Test Career Record: Bowling							
Balls	Runs	Wkts	Avg	Best	5WI	10WM	BPW
2400	1124	33	34.06	5-40	1	0	72.72

Overseas tours: WI 90/91, 94/95, SL 92/93, 94/95, NZ 92/93, 94/95, Eng 93, SA 93/94, Pak 94/95, Sharjah 93/94, WC: NZ 91/92

Test matches: Eng 90/91 (2), WI 90/91 (5), Ind 91/92 (4), SL 92/93 (3), WI 92/93 (5), NZ 92/93 (2), Eng 93 (6), NZ 93/94 (3), SA 93/94 (3), SA 93/94 (3), Pak 94/95 (3), Eng 94/95 (5)

Highest score against each country:			100s	50s
England	140	Brisbane 94/95	3	7
India	34	Melbourne 91/92	0	0
New Zealand	111	Hobart 93/94	1	1
Pakistan	71	Lahore 94/95	0	3
South Africa	113*	Durban 93/94	1	1
Sri Lanka	56	Colombo 92/93	0	1
West Indies	139*	St John's 90/91	2	4

Coopers & Lybrand world rating (batting): 15 (652)

Player Profiles

STEVE WAUGH

Full name: Stephen Rodger Waugh
Born: 02/06/65   Canterbury, Sydney, New South Wales
Country: Australia
Right-hand middle order batsman - Right-arm medium bowler
Test debut: 26/12/85 v India - Melbourne Cricket Ground

Test Career Record: *Batting & Fielding*								
Mat	Inns	N/O	Runs	H/S	Avg	100s	50s	Cat
72	111	21	4011	177*	44.56	7	24	53

Test Career Record: *Bowling*							
Balls	Runs	Wkts	Avg	Best	5WI	10WM	BPW
5761	2574	67	38.41	5-28	3	0	85.98

Overseas tours: NZ 85/86, 89/90, 91/92, 92/93, 94/95, Ind 86/87, 89/90, Pak 88/89, 94/95, Eng 89, 93, WI 90/91, 94/95, SA 93/94, SL 94/95, Sharjah 85/86, 86/87, 93/94, WC: Ind & Pak 87/88, NZ 91/92, Aus B: Zim 91/92, Young Aus: Zim 85/86

Test matches: Ind 85/86 (2), NZ 85/86 (3), Ind 86/87 (3), Eng 86/87 (5), NZ 87/88 (3), Eng 87/88 (1), SL 87/88 (1), Pak 88/89 (3), WI 88/89 (5), Eng 89 (6), NZ 89/90 (1), SL 89/90 (2), Pak 89/90 (3), NZ 89/90 (1), Eng 90/91 (3), WI 90/91 (2), WI 92/93 (5), NZ 92/93 (3), Eng 93 (6), NZ 93/94 (3), SA 93/94 (1), SA 93/94 (3), Pak 94/95 (2), Eng 94/95 (5)

Highest score against each country:			100s	50s
England	177*	Headingley 89	3	9
India	39*	Delhi 86/87	0	0
New Zealand	147*	Brisbane 93/94	1	5
Pakistan	98	Rawalpindi 94/95	0	3
South Africa	164	Adelaide 93/94	1	2
Sri Lanka	134*	Hobart 89/90	1	2
West Indies	100	Sydney 92/93	1	3

Coopers & Lybrand world rating (batting): 5= (758)

KEPLER WESSELS

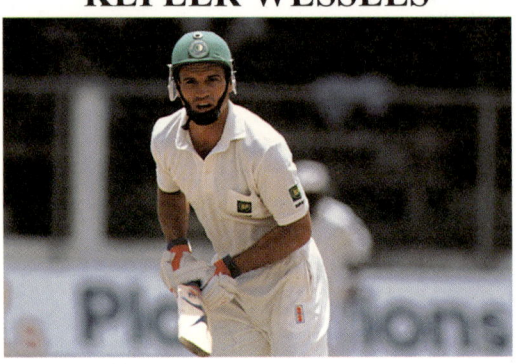

Full name: Kepler Christoffel Wessels
Born: 14/09/57   Bloemfontein, South Africa
Country: South Africa
Left-hand opening batsman - Right-arm medium or Off break bowler
Test debuts: 26/11/82 v England - Woolloongabba, Brisbane (Australia)
18/04/92 v West Indies - Kensington Oval, Bridgetown (South Africa)

Test Career Record: *Batting & Fielding*									
Mat	Inns	N/O	Runs	H/S	Avg	100s	50s	Cat	
24	42	1	1761	179	42.95	4	9	18	Aus
16	29	2	1027	118	38.03	2	6	12	S/A
40	71	3	2788	179	41.00	6	15	30	Total

Test Career Record: *Bowling (Aus)*							
Balls	Runs	Wkts	Avg	Best	5WI	10WM	BPW
90	42	0	-	-	-	-	-

Overseas tours: With Australia: SL 82/83, WI 83/84, Ind 84/85, Eng 85, Sharjah 84/85, WC: Eng 83

With South Africa: Ind 91/92, 93/94, WI 91/92, SL 93/94, Aus 93/94, Eng 94, Pak 94/95, WC: Aus & NZ 91/92

Test matches: For Australia: Eng 82/83 (4), SL 82/83 (1), Pak 83/84 (5), WI 83/84 (2), WI 84/85 (5), Eng 85 (6), NZ 85/86 (1)

For South Africa: WI 91/92 (1), Ind 92/93 (4), SL 93/94 (3), Aus 93/94 (2), Aus 93/94 (3), Eng 94 (3)

Highest score against each country:			100s	50s
Australia	63*	Melbourne 93/94 S/A	0	2
England	162	Brisbane 82/83 Aus	2	4
India	118	Durban 92/93 S/A	1	1
New Zealand	70	Brisbane 85/86 Aus	0	1
Pakistan	179	Adelaide 83/84 Aus	1	0
Sri Lanka	141	Kandy 82/83 Aus	1	1
West Indies	173	Sydney 84/85 Aus	1	6

Coopers & Lybrand world rating (batting): 34 (554)

CRAIG WHITE

Full name: Craig White
Born: 16/12/69   Morley, Yorkshire, England
Country: England
Right-arm medium bowler - Right-hand middle order batsman
Test debut: 02/06/94 v New Zealand - Trent Bridge, Nottingham

Test Career Record: *Batting & Fielding*								
Mat	Inns	N/O	Runs	H/S	Avg	100s	50s	Cat
4	6	0	131	51	21.83	0	1	3

Test Career Record: *Bowling*							
Balls	Runs	Wkts	Avg	Best	5WI	10WM	BPW
469	258	8	32.25	3-18	0	0	58.62

Overseas tours: Aus 94/95, Young Eng: WI 89/90

Test matches: NZ 94 (3), SA 94 (1)

Best bowling against each country:			5WI	10WM
New Zealand	3-18	Old Trafford 94	0	0
South Africa	2-43	Lord's 94	0	0

Coopers & Lybrand world rating (bowling): 70 (137*)

Player Profiles

GUY WHITTALL

Full name: Guy James Whittall
Born: 05/09/72   Chipinga (Chipinge), Zimbabwe
Country: Zimbabwe
Right-hand middle order batsman - Right-arm medium bowler
Test debut: 01/12/93 v Pakistan - Defence Stadium, Karachi

Test Career Record: Batting & Fielding								
Mat	*Inns*	*N/O*	*Runs*	*H/S*	*Avg*	*100s*	*50s*	*Cat*
9	13	2	304	113*	27.63	1	1	5
Test Career Record: Bowling								
Balls	*Runs*	*Wkts*	*Avg*	*Best*	*5WI*	*10WM*		*BPW*
1434	588	18	32.66	4-70	0	0		79.66

Overseas tours: Eng 93, Pak 93/94, Aus 94/95

Test matches: Pak 93/94 (3), SL 94/95 (3), Pak 94/95 (3)

Highest score against each country:		100s	50s
Pakistan	113 * Harare 94/95	1	0
Sri Lanka	61 * Harare 94/95	0	1

Coopers & Lybrand world rating (batting): 78 (296*)